THE PRIVATE EYE ANNUAL 1999

EDITED BY IAN HISLOP

Published in Great Britain by
Private Eye Productions Ltd
6 Carlisle Street, London W1V 5RG

© 1999 Pressdram Ltd
ISBN 1 901784 142
Designed by Bridget Tisdall
Printed in England by
Ebenezer Baylis & Son Ltd, Worcester

2 4 6 8 10 9 7 5 3 1

THE PRIVATE EYE ANNUAL 1999

EDITED BY IAN HISLOP

The Rebranding of Britain Part 94

WHY GENETICALLY MODIFIED ROYALTY IS SO DANGEROUS

by Prince Charles (with help from Jonathon Porridge and Jonathan Dimblebore)

TAMPERING with the genetic base of the Royal Family may result in a whole range of disastrous and unforeseen consequences, say experts.

In recent years scientists have attempted to make the Royal Family more productive by introducing alien genes culled from other species. For example, the introduction of the so-called "Fergienator" gene was made, in the hope of producing a more vivacious, informal, modern breed of Royalty. But the experiment had to be aborted when the Fergie gene went "wild" and hybridised with a number of rogue American strains.

Even more horrific were the results of the notorious Diana experiment, launched in 1981. To begin with, scientists were exultant, claiming huge popularity yields and a surplus of goodwill which they believed would guarantee the survival of the Royal Family well into the next Millennium.

GM THE QUEEN

But after a few years, the externally introduced gene "ran amok", nearly wiping out the entire Royal Family for ever.

The moral of this tragic saga of thoughtless interference with God's natural scheme is only too obvious. The Royal Family must be allowed to cross-pollinate only with traditional English stock, such as the time-honoured Camelia Parker-

bowlensis, a delightful evergreen shrub which can be seen in the beds at Highgrove throughout the year.

The Daily Pornograph

Britain's biggest-selling quality daily

(1 million copies given away on trains)

Comment by Charles Phwoar, Editor of The Daily Pornograph
(formerly the Daily Hellograph, formerly the Daily Hurleygraph)

Clinton — It *Is* An Immoral Issue

VARIOUS liberal commentators have argued that the details of the sexual shenanigans indulged in by President Clinton (see Full-Colour Pull-Out, only in today's soaraway Daily Pornograph) are in some way a side issue from the real problems facing America and the world. Nothing could be further from the truth. Mr Clinton's sex life *is* an immoral issue, thank God — and so is this issue of the Daily Telegraph. If you're keen to read words such as "smear", "stain", "grope", "genitalia" and "Ambrose Evans-Pritchard" then this is the paper for you! Enjoy!

©The Dirty Telegraph

In Tomorrow's Telegraph
- Perjury is a serious offence for which the President must not be forgiven **2**
- Why is Jonathan Aitken being persecuted for telling a little white lie to protect his family? **3**

That Clinton Prayer Breakfast In Full

Waffle with syrup

— ✳ —

Freshly squeezed tears

— ✳ —

Humble pie (off)

"You spoil those lemmings"

GLENDA SLAGG

Fleet Street's Millennium Dame!

FOR Gawd's sake, Mr Starr, give our Bill a break!?! Yes, you, Mr Witch Finder General, with your holier-than-thou smirk and your 36 bible-bashin' boxes of bonkin' bollox!!! ('Scuse me, Mr Editor, but that's what it is!) You're starr-ting to be a pain in the neck! We know your type, a-creepin' and a-peepin' through the keyhole to watch poor old Bill and his buxom bimbo having a bit of fun!? Clear off back to the Starr-chamber (Geddit?!?!) and leave an innocent man to smoke his cigar in peace!!!?

BILL CLINTON!! What a slimy, low down, two-timin' lyin' cheatin' two timer! If I was Hillary I'd shove his ten-cent cigar up his you-know-where?!?! And I'd advise the American people to do the same!!?!?! All together now: "Hit the Road, Bill, and doncha come back no more no more no more" *(That's enough "no mores". Ed.)*

MONICA Lewinsky!! What a Grade A Bitch!!!?? Don't play the innocent with me, little Miss Trailer Trash!?! Poor old Bill didn't know what hit him when Moanin' Monica came a-lustin' and a-bustin' into the Oval Office!??! Don't blame the President, Mr Media Men, blame the gal with the Thong at Twilight!! Geddit??!?

I SAY shed a tear for poor Monica Lewinsky!?!?! She was a small time gal from way out west who didn't stand a chance in the big bad city when wicked Willie came a-leerin' and a-smearin' into her lonesome little life!!?! Let's face it, gals, all fellas are the same!! They're bastards!!! And the sooner they resign the better for all of us!?!

Here they are, Glenda's All-Starr Bastards!?!?! (Shurely "Sex Bombs"? Ed.)

● AL GORE — He may be dull, he may love his wife, but I reckon he's Al man! Gore blimey!! (Geddit?!?)

● GORE VIDAL — He may be gay and over the hill, but he's still got one Vidal statistic I like the sound of! Gore Blimey!! *(You've done this. Ed.)*

● AMBROSE EVANS PRITCHARD — Crazy name, completely crazy guy!!

Byeeee!!

6

Why Clinton Must Go

by William Rees-Mogg

MISS MONICA Lewinsky is just a side show in the grand drama that is now unfolding on the banks of the Potomac.

That the President is an adulterer and a liar is serious but not critical. After all, this has been true of every President I have known personally over the past 50 years.

No, what will force the resignation of President Jefferson Clintesterone will be the fact that he is a serial mass-murderer and for the past 20 years has been simply the front man for one of the biggest Mafia-controlled drug-laundering operations in the Western world, run by notorious Arkansas hoodlums such as Charlie "the Coyote" Horsebox Whittington-Smythe and others of his ilk.

His wife Hilary Roddam Clintoris, I am told on very good authority, was for many years a "hooker" in one of the leading "establishments" in downtown Little Rock.

The two of them also had a lucrative sideline in running guns to the IRA.

I know all this because some chap told me all about it in the gents at the Garrick. I am sure he knew what he was talking about, because his father was at Charterhouse with me in the 1920s.

© Lord Really-Smugg

Daily Mail
COMMENT

A Year On — Was It Just A Case Of Mass Hysteria?

asks Lynda Lee-Slagg, A.N. Wislon, John Mortiboys, etc, etc

WAS IT all a dream? Did we all take leave of our senses? Did the media whip us up into a state of misplaced emotional frenzy which bore no relation to reality?

Just over a year later, it is difficult to believe that we were all so uncritical. That we were prepared to elevate to semi-divine status an ordinary flawed human being whose compassionate smile often disguised the manipulative and ruthless personality beneath.

It is time to get on with our lives. We must stop going on about Tony Blair as if he was some sort of saint. In fact (cont'd. p. 94)

How it will look: The new scaled-down Diana Memorial Garden

EMPEROR TO LAUNCH NEW CLOTHES RANGE

by Our Fairy Tale Staff **Will Self-Publicist**

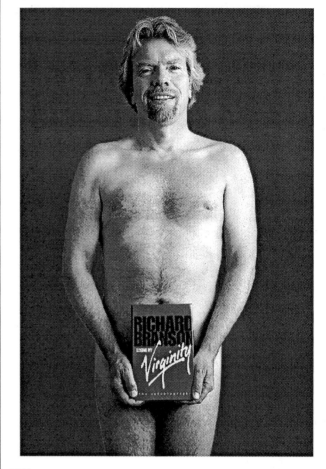

THE EMPEROR of Business today revealed his fabulous new range of high-quality clothing. The fashion market is a new departure for the multi-talented Emperor who has so far turned to gold all that he has touched.

Says the Emperor, "This suit I am wearing is certain to catch on. It is woven of the finest thread and cut in the latest style. Everyone will be flocking to my shops."

However, one onlooker, a small boy in the crowd, pointed out that the Emperor was entirely naked and that his clothes were on a par with his trains, ie they were non-existent.

"Still working for the Open University?"

The Coming Revolution That Is Going To Change Britain's Politics Forever

The Third Woy

by Our Constitutional Staff Vernon Bogdasnore

MAKE no mistake! Politics will never be the same again when elder statesman Lord Jenkins of Halfdead delivers his long-awaited 8,500 page invitation to lunch at the Garrick Club *(surely 'report on how to reform Britain's voting procedures?' Ed.)*.

Lord Jenkins is expected to consider a number of methods of proportional representation.

These include STV (the Single Transferable Vote), AV (Alternative Voting), MLV (Multiple List Voting) and HMG (Her Majesty's Government to stay in power forever under the enlightened leadership of TB).

Lord Jenkins is expected to come down in favour of a form of HMG, a system already in successful use in such countries as Malaysia, North Korea and Cuba.

However, he may recommend that the HMG system should only be adopted so long as it includes an element of LDC (Liberal Democratic Coalition) which involves a permanent seat at the Garrick for Lord Jenkins *(surely 'a seat in the Cabinet for Mr Ashdown'? Ed.)*.

Said one leading constitutional expert, "There is the first-past-the-post system, there is PR and then there is this ludicrous idea — The Third Woy".

Lord Jenkins is 107.

"We're trying for another baby"

M. Buerk: ...and now, for the latest on the great Russian crisis, we go over to Our Chief Global Affairs Editor John Simpson in Moscow.

(Cut to smug looking man in grey overcoat, sitting in front of picture of Kremlin)

Buerk: John, it seems things are looking black for Russia tonight?

Simpson: Yes, Michael, I think the best way to sum up the situation here in Russia tonight is that it is looking pretty black. I was speaking earlier today to one of the most influential members of the Duma, Alexander Middleoftheroadski, leader of the hardline Liberal Social Democratic Nationalist party.

(Film of Simpson nodding earnestly as man in suit drones on)

Russian: I think situation here in Moskva is best described in one old Russian phrase: is looking pretty black.

Simpson: There you have it. The situation has now reached a point which almost all commentators are describing as "pretty black". This is John Simpson, about to go off and write a long piece for the Sunday Telegraph, in Moscow.

Buerk: Thank you, John. And now, back to our main story of the evening, Viagra, does it cause BSE?

"WHY I HATE THE PRESS"

MEL FAT talks exclusively to all newspapers

"HOW dare you interview me?"

Mel Fat is not pleased at my first question, "Mr Fat, why are you so marvellous?"

"Do you know how important I am?" he shouts. "I am the director of the greatest film ever made, *Mr Bore*. I've made huge amounts of money."

At first sight Mel Fat appears a deeply unpleasant man. But at second sight he does as well.

"God, I hate the British press," he tells me, lighting a cigar. "They don't understand my genius. They think I'm just some TV comic because I invite them round to plug my new TV comedy series. The fact is that I'm the world's greatest director — why can't you miserable jealous journos acknowledge this? Now get out."

Mel Fat stars in the *Fat and Thin Show* with Gryff Rhys-Thin starting on BBC One on Wednesday.

Introducing the Eye's Exciting New Columnist

POLLY FILLER

THIS morning the nanny was late. Again. Charlie, my two year old began screaming. My partner was no help, because he had stayed out half the night, watching the football with his friends.

Sometimes I think he's a bigger baby than the baby. Anyway, I knew it was going to be one of those days.

"Why are you late?" I said to the nanny, when she finally came through the door.

I was seriously annoyed because I was planning to meet a friend at Peter Jones to look at sofas — though why I want to buy another sofa for Charlie to be sick all over is beyond me.

At this point, Simon, my partner, finally appeared from upstairs.

"I'm having a terrible morning," he said. "My computer's crashed and now I've lost one of my contact lenses."

"What about me?" I said. "The nanny's late, and I was meant to be meeting Liz to look at sofas in Peter Jones."

"I'm sorry I'm so late," the nanny lamely explained. "I've been up all night with my father who's dying."

"Shut up and stop whingeing," Simon and I both said simultaneously.

Then we laughed. Thank goodness we agree about some things.

© *All newspapers.*

THAT STARR INVESTIGATION

IN FULL

Q: Would you please state your full name for the record?

Starr: Kenneth Torquemada Ringo Starr III.

Q: Mr Starr, did you or did you not screw the President?

Starr: I did not, sir.

Q: Did you *try* and screw the President?

Starr: I have no memory of that, sir.

Q: I put it to you, Mr Starr, that you wanted his ass.

Starr: It depends what you mean by his ass.

Q: You wanted to shaft him, didn't you?

Starr: I did not, sir.

Q: You abused your position of authority to harass him, then you cornered him in his office and grabbed him by the short and curlies.

Starr: That is not my recollection, sir.

Q: Do you not admit that this was an inappropriate investigation?

Starr: I have done nothing wrong.

Q: You interfered with the President's evidence, didn't you?

Starr: I deny that.

Q: Let's face it, Mr Starr, you wanted the President "fucked".

Starr: It depends on your definition of the word "fucked". It is my belief that since the President *is* not and has not been completely fucked by me, then it follows that I did not go the whole way.

Q: Are you saying you did *not* have sexual revelations?

Starr: I do not deny that sexual revelations took place, but I stand by my earlier statement. Whatever it was.

Q: At the very least, Mr Starr, you wanted to do "a job" on the President.

Starr: That is a personal matter between me and Mr Clinton.

Q: Is it not true that on 21st September 1998 the President was on his knees in front of you?

Starr: That is...

Q: And you had him by the balls?

Starr: I did not.

(At this point the reader gets up and goes to the restroom to have a much needed bath after reading this stuff)

In the wake of the Lewinsky Affair **Dr Thomas Utterfraud** asks "Is the Editor just a sex addict?"

THE CLINTON affair raises important medical issues, not the least of which concerns the emotional and mental health of the most powerful man in the Times. Many editors seek solace in sex stories and could be said to be sex-aholics, needing sex stories once or twice a page to keep them satisfied. However, their demand for constant stimulation can lead them to errors of judgement in which sexual titillation assumes a higher priority than any other activity such as politics, economics or the Liberal Democrat Conference in Brighton (cont. p. 69)

The Editor couldn't get enough

FOOD SCARE – LATEST

by **Old Trevor Macdonald**

THE PUBLIC are being advised by the government not to swallow any more food scares, as they may end up feeling anxious and depressed.

The food scares can be found in most newspapers and contain large quantities of BSE, CJD, E-Coli or Crohn's Disease. In severe cases, the consumption of excess food scares can lead to hysteria, madness and the end of agriculture.

(Reuters)

I Say Leave Clinton Alone

by **Polly Technic** (now the University of Toynbee)

WHEN are people going to grow up, and stop going on as though sex was important?

Clinton's fumblings with some silly young floozie in his office have got nothing to do with serious, adult politics.

It is time to leave the leader of the Free World to get on with the job we all elected him to do — ie, carrying out the liberal, progressive, forward-looking agenda that is supported by every right-thinking person on the left: eg, setting up medicare, defending the right to choose, and bombing the hell out of Third World aspirin factories in the hope of diverting attention from his private life.

"I'm leaving you, Gerald – don't try and stop me!"

"You're quite right — I am using the wrong service sheet"

Private Eye's exclusive serialisation of the world's most important book, *Why I Hate Mrs Thatcher* by the Rt Hon Sir Edward Heath PC, MP

Chapter One: How I Hate Mrs Thatcher

I SHALL never forget the day, ever, when I lost the Party leadership to that dreadful woman who stabbed me in the back after I had plucked her from obscurity and made her Minister of Paperclips. And how did she repay me? Bloody cow! She only goes and refuses to give me a job — just because I told her I wouldn't take a job from her even if she offered it to me on her bended knee!

Chapter Two: Why I Never Got Married

ONE OF the most important historical questions about my premiership is why I never married.

The explanation, I can now reveal, is that although the names of many women were suggested to me, including that of the well-known pianist Daniel Baremboim, it was out of the question that I could marry any of them for the very good reason that I was already deeply in love with someone else, ie myself.

Those Commonwealth Games Results In Full

(continued from p. 1)

Shooting

Water Cannon, 200 metres
1. Malaysia

Rubber Bullets, 5 metres
1. Malaysia

Live Ammunition, point blank
1. Malaysia

Street Running

4 x 400 metres
1. Malaysian Crowd
2. Malaysian Police

Throwing The Canister (Tear Gas)
1. Malaysian Police
2. Malaysian Crowd

Smiling And Pretending That Nothing Is Happening (3-Day Event)
1. H.M. The Queen (England)
2. Mahatir Mohammad (Malaysia)

School Announcements

St Cakes

Meltdown Term begins today. There are only seven boys in the school, due to the unforeseen collapse of the Malaysian, Indonesian, Thai, Hong Kong and Russian economies. P.M.W. Footsie (Hundred's) is Head of Derivatives. Hang Seng (Index's) is Keeper of the Bear Market. D.O.W. Jones (Salomon's) is Captain of the Wall Street Game. Owing to financial difficulties there are no staff this year. The Rev. P.D. O'Phile (Chaplain 1983-94) has been released back into the community and returns as Director of Internet Studies of the Lower School. The new Detoxification Wing (formerly the School Library) will be opened by Miss Paula Yates (OC) and her current partner (TBA). There will be a performance of Sir Harrison Birtwistle's *Panic* by the School Orchestra at "Last Night Of The Cakes" on 5 November (tickets from the Bursar, Brigadier K.G.B. Zhirinovsky at Dunyeltsin, College Road). Suicides will be on 10 December.

Freshers' week circa 1650

- *Queen Mother "liked" Thatcher*
- *Thatcher "couldn't stand" the Queen*
- *The Queen "loved" horses*

THE WYFRONT DIARIES

ALREADY everybody is talking about them as the most sensational literary event of the decade. For over 40 years the late Woodrow Wyfront occupied a key position in British life as head of the Horserace Totalisator Board, rubbing shoulders with all the greatest horses of our age. But only now has it come to light that, throughout that time, Lord Wyfront was keeping a daily diary, chronicling the intrigues, the scandals, the glitter, the glatter and the glotter of his charmed circle. Now read on:

1979 May 21: Lunch at the Garrick with William (Rees-Mogg) and Bernard (Levin). They tell me, on the highest authority, that some new woman has been put in charge at Number 10. Her name apparently is Thatcher. Can't see that lasting.

June 1: Had one of my famous "lunches" with Bernard and a glittering array of the

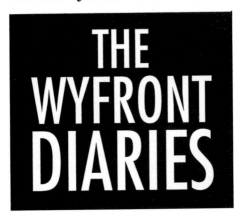

Marquesa Bettina di Coronatione Strada - a close friend of Lord Wyfront

WHO'S WHO IN THE WORLD OF WOODROW WYFRONT

Mrs Thatcher: Prime Minister of Britain 1979-1990.

Her Majesty the Queen: Queen of England since 1952.

Lord Really-Smugg: formerly William Rees-Mogg, one of Wyfront's oldest friends.

"Honest Jock" Balon: one of the most respected bookmakers of his time.

Lady Moussaka Wyfront: Greek-born 14th wife of the celebrated diarist.

Salmonella Wyfront: beautiful, talented daughter of the celebrated diarist, and known in her own right as his daughter.

Sid Wingfield-Digby: manager of local branch of Sketchley's, responsible for cleaning Lord Wyfront's celebrated collection of bow ties.

rich and powerful. They included the Queen Mother, a dear woman, looking radiant as always. We discussed who was going to win the Derby. How knowledgeable she is about horses.

June 29: Lunch at the Athenaeum with a very important man, whose name I cannot disclose or even remember. I was able to tell him that I had heard on the very highest authority that it was a warm day. Enjoyed a cigar with the brandy.

August 12: A historic day. I have been summoned to lunch at Chequers by Mrs Thatcher. She was very pleased with my reference to her in my News of the World column as "the greatest and most beautiful woman I have ever had the honour to meet". I told her that she should not be afraid to run the country in any way she wants. She said she valued my advice, because I was never afraid to speak my mind.

1983. November 21: Dinner at George Weidenfeld's. The food as usual was uneatable and the conversation tedious beyond belief. Ted Heath was there, looking radiant. He told me that he had once been Prime Minister.

1987. June 12: Gave one of my famous lunches in honour of my very old friend the Queen Mother. "You are looking very radiant, your Majesty," I told her in my blunt outspoken way. Over the Lobster Thermidor she confided in me that her daughter was the Queen of England, and what did I advise? I said I would mention it in my column in the News of the World. She was very pleased.

1990. November 22: My very oldest friend Mrs Thatcher couldn't come to lunch because she has been cruelly cast aside by her Party. "This is indeed a black day", as I confided to her on the telephone, when she rang to tell me the news. Took my favourite purple bow tie with the yellow polka dots to the cleaners. They promised to have it back to me in time for Ascot, where I may well have the honour of meeting the Queen.

NEXT WEEK: I have lunch with Lord Weinstock, a man called Major becomes Prime Minister and I get my bow tie back from the cleaners.

"It's from the University of Life... You didn't get in"

MURDOCH'S MAN UTD BID BLOCKED

This will in no way influence my view of Tony Blair — the two-faced snivelling little shit...

IN THE COURTS

Judge Accused of £1 Million Mortgage Swindle

Regina v. Mr Justice Fraud

Before Mr Justice Cocklecarrot

Sir Hartley Redface Q.C. *(for the accused)*: M'lud, I submit that were this trial to proceed, my client, who is already a very sick man, might well go out of his mind and be tempted to take his own life.

Mr Justice Cocklecarrot *(for it is he)*: This is indeed distressing news. The defendant, who is of course well known to me as a fellow member of the Garrick Club, has indeed been of unsound mind, to my certain knowledge, for many years. Sir Hartley, have you any evidence to support your plea, true though it undoubtedly is?

Sir Hartley: I would like to call a very eminent psychiatrist, Sir Ephraim Redface.

Sir Ephraim: Seldom have I encountered such a clear case of what we psychiatrists call *Dementia Judicalis*, or *Saunders' Syndrome*, as it is commonly known to the layman. In my expert view, were these unfortunate proceedings against my brother's client to continue, Mr Justice Fraud might well be found guilty, which would undoubtedly be gravely detrimental to his balance of mind.

Cocklecarrot: Not to mention his balance of bank!

(Laughter)

Sir Hartley: Indeed M'lud. And, on that matter, may I suggest that it would help my client to retain his sanity were his

salary to continue to be paid, in addition to the generous support of the legal aid board which has enabled my own fees to be paid in this matter.

Cocklecarrot: As you wish, Sir Hartley. I therefore suggest that the Crown submit a plea of *nolle prosequi*, so that we can all go off to luncheon at the Garrick.

(The case was concluded)

SALLY JOCKSTRAP
The Voice of Sport

WHO is going to land the coveted Tottenham Wednesday job? Come on, Will Carling — say yes or no! My money is on Billy Graham anyway!

WHAT'S gone wrong with our tennis players? Why are there no British boys in the top 5? They are all foreigners like Tim Henman and Greg Norman! Pull your socks up, Sports Minister, Frankie de Tory, and do something before the next World Cup!

SEND the Ref off! The way the one on Saturday fell over when the Italian player gave him a push was a disgrace! Our national game is being undermined by drugtaking. Come on, Des Lynam, take a stand!

BY THE way, copies of my new book about the World Cup, Belgium 96, will soon be on sale. It unfortunately had to be pulped because there was a picture of a cricket match on the cover.

Letter to The Guardian

As a young person I have recently discovered that there was a huge war between 1914 and 1918 in which millions of people were killed.

Why is this event consistently ignored in Britain? Surely we should remember this horrendous event and perhaps build some sort of memorial to commemorate the fallen.

I would be prepared to go on a sponsored walk to raise money for such a scheme.

Also, are there any books or videos or designated websites about this war? No one seems to want to write anything about it, which is pretty shocking.

Simon Simple,
2nd Year History student
at the University of Styrene
(formerly Styrene Poly)

What You Will Not See In

VIAGRA MAN BONKS 200 TIMES A NIGHT AND WINS DIGITAL DECODER

Friday, October 16, 1998

RAUNCHY RUPE'S TASTY CHINESE TAKEAWAY!

By Sun Staff CHRIS MUCK and TREVOR FILTH

THE DIRTY Digger's at it again!

Only a few weeks after multi-media magnate Rupe Murdoch walked out on his bride of 27 years, he has helped himself to a right little Prawn Cracker from Peking!

She is curvaceous, busty Wendy Deng, a pint-sized sex kitten from the Orient.

When the saucy siren from Shanghai caught the Dirty Digger's eye at a glitzy Manhattan book-launch, it was a case of lust at first sight!

Porn Cracker

Neighbours in their exclusive Upper East Side apartment block said last night "they are at it night and day".

But while Abo Rupe is busy showing off his legendary didgeridoo to the Suzie Wong who can't get enough, 3000 miles away in California his estranged wife Liz is plotting her revenge.

Last night she told the Sun: "I'm going to sue that bastard for every penny he's got."

A case of chop suey, wouldn't you say Rupe?

ON OTHER PAGES	*Plus*	*Plus*
Lusty Liz Murdoch is back on Freud's Couch (and she's mad for it!) p. 8	Why the euro is good for British business p. 16	Don't watch Sky, it's rubbish! says TV critic Gary p. 94

St Crumpets Ladies' College

(An independent girls' school affiliated to St Cakes)

Celebrity Term begins today. There are 307 daughters of famous people in the school. Lourdes Madonna (Virgins) is Head of Pop. Poshella Beckham (Ziggers) is Victoria Ludorum. Melella B. (Zaggers) is Captain of Spices. Miss E.R.L. Tweed-Skirt has retired as Matron. She is replaced by Miss V.D. Tongue-Stud who takes responsibility for body piercing and tattoos. All Saints Day will be celebrated on Nov. 12th when there will be a rendition of the school song "Never Ever" *(shurely Floreat Crumpetana?)*. Discs will be played on the Upper Downer on 17th March. Slappers are on Dec. 12th.

THEATRE

The Blue Movie Room
by David Pubic-Hare (adapted from La Bonque by Wiener Schnitzler)

Reviewed by Charles Spencer

PHWOAR! Blimey! Cor! That Nicole Kidman! Wouldn't you? I bet you would! Phwoar!

Pop Porn
by Ben Elton Johnson

Reviewed by Charles Spencer

PHWOAR! Blimey! Cor! That Emma Noble! Wouldn't you? I bet you would! I wish I was James Major! Phwoar!

© The Daily Pornograph and all other newspapers

Late News

FURY AS ULSTER KILLERS SET FREE

THERE was uproar in Republican circles at the news that two soldiers who had murdered an innocent civilian were to be released. Said a Sinn Fein spokesman, "This is a disgrace. These men are murderers and they are being allowed to escape Scott free. What sort of message does" (cont. p. 94)

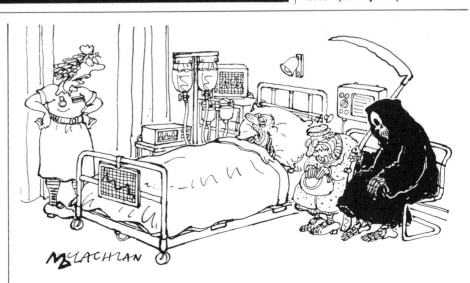

*"You know the rules, Mr Dotterill — you're only allowed **one** visitor at a time."*

13

NEWS

Important Video Launch

■ Hollywood company launches new video about Titanic disaster, starring Leonardo DiCaprio and Britain's Kate Winslet . . . . **Page 1**

Titanic hit

■ New film set to break all records as top-selling video of all time . . .**Page 2**

Queue the action

■ There were mile-long queues last night outside video shops all over Britain, as crazed teenagers and old-aged pensioners, not to mention middle-aged persons and small dogs, fought to get their hands on the award-winning new Titanic video, produced by 20th Century Fox . . . .**Page 3**

BUSINESS

Winner for Murdoch: Fox shares should soar to new high on record video sales, says Times City editor R. Slicker . . . .**Page 38**

COLUMNS

MATTHEW PARRIS
Is Leonardo the most beautiful man in the world (apart from Rupert Murdoch)? . . . . **Page 28**

Eager shoppers queue to purchase the Titanic video

WILLIAM REES-MOGG
I do not have a video device, but if I did, rest assured, this is the only film I would want to see . . . .**Page 28**

SIMON JENKINS
Why I say Titanic video could be answer to Middle East crisis . . . .**Page 28**

ALAN COREN
News of Titanic sinking reaches Cricklewood — "They said it was unthinkable — but it seems to have thunk." . . . .**Page 28**

FASHION

Hemlines sink to new low — the Titanic look is in! . . . .**Page 14**

SPORT

Snooker: All the top seeds in this year's Embassy tournament will probably fail to turn up because they will be at home watching the new Titanic video . . . .**Page 64**

BOOKS

No one is buying any books because they are far too busy watching the hugely entertaining new video Titanic .**Page 68**

MEDICAL NOTES

Dr Thomas Uttafraud on how watching videos can improve your sex-life (particularly if they happen to feature top British stars such as Kate Winslet) . . . .**Page 70**

PLUS

A special souvenir pull-out newspaper giving the day's other news, free with every copy of your 108-page Times-tanic.

OBITUARY

The Times . . . .**Page 84**

CROSSWORD

ACROSS
1. Ship that sank in famous video (7)

DOWN
1. Scrambled it antic makes terrific video from 20th Century Fox (7)

First correct entry wins free copy of new award-winning video, to "Times Titanic Offer", PO Box 999, Virginia Street, E1.

YES — IT'S THE PEOPLE'S PARLIAMENT

by Our Political Staff **Conrad Blackrod and Peter Garter-Ruck**

IN THE biggest shake-up of Parliamentary procedure since records were kept, the so-called State Opening of Parliament has been totally remodelled to bring it into line with the world of the internet and the euro.

At Her Majesty the Queen's personal request, the ceremony has been cut from four and a half hours to four hours 25 minutes.

Out go all the bygone rituals and mediaeval flummeries which have made the opening of Britain's parliament the laughing stock of the world.

For example, you will no longer see the Grand Golden Spoon of the Wardrobe (Brigadier Anstruther-Wapshott) walking backwards in front of the Queen, as she is presented with the Silver Handbag containing her Government's speech. Instead he will present the speech in an ordinary briefcase, while crawling forwards on all floors.

Many of the dignitaries traditionally included in the procession from the Great Lobby to the steps of the Speaker's Chamber have now been relegated to watching the proceedings from the Distinguished Peers Gallery.

Those affected include the Warden of the Portcullis Poursuivant (Lord Ferret), the Master of the Green Carpet (Air Vice-Marshal Sir Terence Tubbie) and the Third Stick in Waiting (Lady Petunia Starborgling).

In a bid to slash the escalating cost of the ceremony, Her Majesty has given permission for the State Opening to be sponsored by Virgin Trains, who have insisted that the Queen should make the journey from Buckingham Palace by rail, via Manchester Piccadilly, Stockport and Macclesfield Parkway (buffet facilities not available).

STOP PRESS

State Opening of Parliament delayed by four hours, due to "wrong kind of trains on the track" p. 42

IN CASE OF CEASEFIRE BREAK LEGS

TRIUMPH FOR COOK AS SAS ARREST WORLD'S MOST HATED WAR CRIMINAL

by Our Security Staff **Alastair Campbell**

IN THE most daring top-secret paramilitary operation ever mounted, a crack squad of SAS-style policemen (Inspector "Knacker of the Yard" Knacker) carried out a midnight swoop to arrest the world's most hated mass-murderer, General Augustus Pinochet.

Said a triumphant Knacker, "This was an immaculately co-ordinated operation, requiring months of planning and split-second timing."

"Acting on a tip-off from a Daily Mail newspaper headline *Pinochet In Britain*, I arranged to drop round to the premises of the Central London Nursing Home For Distressed Fascist Gentlemen at precisely 00 hundred hours, armed with a warrant from a Spanish judge, José Cocklecarrotos.

"When I entered the clinic, all was quiet, apart from the snoring of another Fascist gentleman in an adjacent room, a Mr Hitler from Germany."

All's Well That Allende's Well

"Within seconds, I was at the former dictator's bedside. He immediately attempted to escape, by feigning sleep.

"You don't fool me," I told him. "You're nicked."

Foreign Secretary Robin Cook was quick to praise Inspector Knacker, and himself, for the daring capture of one of the world's most wanted men.

"Let this be a warning," he said, "to mass-murderers like Slobodan Milosevic. If they ever come to England for medical treatment and have tea with Mrs Thatcher, we shall be waiting for them — so long as we have the appropriate warrant from the Spanish authorities."

General Pinochet is 106.

Mad Thatcher's Tea Party

Mad Thatcher's Tea Party

PINOCHET IN THATCHER SHOCK

by Our Diplomatic Staff **Lady Torture**

HUMAN rights activists were appalled yesterday at the news that the world's most hated former right-wing dictator had recently been to tea with General Pinochet.

Said a spokesman, "What sort of message is General Pinochet giving to the world by taking afternoon tea with someone who should be in jail?"

He continued, "Just because Britain supported Chile in the last century, there is no need for the General to compromise his reputation by giving legitimacy to this criminal."

General Pinochet, however, was unrepentant — "I was in London and I suddenly thought I could murder a cup of tea. And then I could make some cake disappear for ever."

That Tea In Full

Coup of Tea

— ✻ —

Rack of Toasted Dissidents

— ✻ —

Grilled Opposition

— ✻ —

Chopped-Off Fingers

— ✻ —

Eggs (Beaten To Death)

— ✻ —

Mrs Teacake

(That's enough Menu. Ed.)

THE TIMES

LETTERS TO THE EDITOR

From Baroness Thatcher, OM
Sir, The arrest of my dear friend General Adolphus Pinochet is an affront to British Justice. This country has a long tradition of giving refuge to war criminals and genocidal despots. Are we going to throw all this away just to satisfy the left-wing do-gooders that make up the current government? If it had not been for Herr Pinochet many British lives would have been lost in the Falklands. Does that not count for something compared to a handful of thousands of Chilean Marxists who committed suicide in an attempt to discredit the Führer?

Surely the right course is to hand over the General to the care of nuns who with the assistance of the Salvation Army can provide a suitable environment for this elderly gentleman to live happily with his memories.
Yours sincerely,
LADY THATCHER,
c/o The Little Sisters of the Rich,
Chester Square,
London.

From Colonel Charles Moore
Sir, Herr Hitler may have been guilty of the death of millions of people, but let us not forget that he brought much needed stability to his country and provided a first class rail service unlike, I might add, the line from Hurst Green to Charing Cross, which was once again late this morning for the fifth time in a week.
Yours sincerely,
COLONEL CHARLES MOORE,
The Old Rectory,
Andrew Robertsbridge.

From The Rt. Hon. Alan Clark MP
Sir, Have we gone stark raving mad? Surely Herr Hitler deserves the endless gratitude of this nation. Without his help by losing, Britain would not have won the 2nd World War.
Whatever happened to loyalty?
Yours sincerely,
THE RT. HON. ALAN CLARK,
Colditz Castle,
Kent.

From Jonathon Boyd Hunta
Sir, Whatever else Neil Hamilton may have done (and we have only his word that he is guilty), he does not deserve to be arrested at midnight, deported to Chile under the orders of the Spanish Junta and then pilloried in the notorious Guardian for the rest of his life.
Yours sincerely,
JONATHON BOYD HUNTA,
Author of "Free the Ritz One — A defence of Mr Christine Hamilton".

"You've wet your bed again, haven't you?"

POETRY CORNER

In Memoriam Eileen Browne, Voice of the BBC's *Listen With Mother*

So. Farewell then
Eileen Browne.
Presenter of
Listen With Mother.

"Are you sitting
Comfortably?"
That was your catchphrase
"Then I'll begin."

But supposing we were not
Sitting comfortably?
How would you have
Known?

> E.J. Thribb (1½)

In Memoriam Anthony Newley, husband of Joan Collins

So. Farewell then
Anthony Newley.
Actor, singer, songwriter,
And director.

*Stop The World,
I Want To Get Off!*

That was your
Greatest hit.

And now
You have!

> E.J. Thribb (17½)
> Poet Laureate Designate

In Memoriam Ernie Wise and Rod Hull

So. Farewell then
Ernie Wise.
You were never the same
Without your partner
Eric Morecambe.

And Emu. How will you
Survive, without
Rod Hull?

That is the
Question.

> E.J. Thribb (17½)

The above poem has been shortlisted for the Walkers Crisps National Poetry Prize. For more details see www.thribbery@aol.com

16

POETRY CORNER

Lines on the decision to correct the perceived sexist approach to women in the James Bond cinematic canon

So. Farewell
Then

The Bond
Girls.

Pussy Galore.
Plenty
O'Toole.

Holly Goodhead.

Those were
Your names.

Who will
Replace you?

Germaine Greer
Suzanne Moore

And Camille
Paglia.

I for one
Cannot wait.

E.J. Womens-Thribb
(0017½)

**In Memoriam
Sir Dirk Bogarde**

So. Farewell
Then.
Sir Dirk
Bogarde.

Actor and
Private Eye
Shareholder.

Yes, you helped
The magazine
Out in the
Sixties.

Keith says that
Was your
Finest hour.

Apart from
*Doctor In The
House.*
Obviously.

E.J. Thribb (17½)

Prince Charming At 50

2000 Friends Attend Grand Ball

by Our Royal Staff **Bad Penny Junor**

AS GUESTS gathered from all over the kingdom to celebrate his 50th birthday, there was general agreement that Prince Charming was entering into a new golden phase of his life which augurs well for the day, we hope still far in the future, when he succeeds to the throne.

As a band of uniformed frogs struck up with a medley of the Prince's favourite songs, including Yin-Tong-Yin-Tong-Diddle-I-Po, the dark shadows seemed at last to have lifted from the Prince's life.

Few now remember the Prince's disastrous marriage to the late Cinderella, Princess of Hearts, which was once described as "a fairytale romance".

Although at the time there was much grief when the Princess died in her coach with the son of the Wicked Sorcerer Ali Baba Fayed, it is now generally accepted in court circles that Cinderella was a manipulative and unscrupulous adventuress, who did Prince Charming serious damage. Everyone now knows that she had an affair with Buttons, her personal footman, and tried to hire the huntsman to kill her love rival in the forest.

Cin-di-rella

And the hostess for the gala evening was none other than that rival, the Prince's longtime consort, Lady Camilla. She of course was one of the so-called ugly sisters and is now recognised as having been the Prince's true love long before the wayward Cinderella made her unfortunate appearance on the scene.

Among those honoured to be present as the new relaxed, mature Prince danced the night away were such Fairyland dignitaries as Sir Stephen Fairy, Sir Nicholas de Soames, the "fattest knight in Christendom", the Lady Candida of the Green, Lord John of Norwich, Lord Hugh Casserole (with his Magic Paintbox) and Mr Squirrel Nutcase, of the Organic Farming and Acupuncture Society.

Among those unfortunately not able to be present was Mr Humpty Dumpster, who recently fell off a wall while drunk, and refused to give a yolk sample to the King's Horses and Men, saying that he had a fear of spoons.

Exclusive to all newspapers

IT HARDLY seems possible. Today is the day when I have to write 50,000 words on Prince Charles. Who would have believed it? It seems like only yesterday that I wrote a piece called "Charles at 40,000 words", although it was actually the day before yesterday.

But today is a very special day — a chance to look back at all the other pieces I've written over the years and reflect on how I can turn them into another very long series of articles to appear all this week.

And what a story it has been. From an uncertain start to a racy middle period to the confidence of maturity, my pieces about Charles have grown in length over the decades until now they stand on the threshold

CHARLES AT FIFTY
THOUSAND WORDS

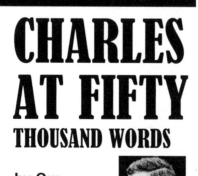

by Our Royal Staff Phil Space

of a new age.

And, of course, this begs several important questions. Is there a future for Prince Charles pieces? How long will they have to go on? Do people really want them? Do they serve any useful function? Should they be replaced by pieces about William? Should I be fired? *(Cont. p. 94)*

Exclusive Recipe
Delia's Perfect Glass of Water

TAKE one glass (preferably made out of glass and without any holes in it) and place under the tap. I find cold water works better than hot — and here's a tip.

Let the cold tap (marked "C") run for a few seconds before filling the glass. Don't forget to turn off the tap when the glass is full — but don't turn it off too soon or you won't have any water.

With practise, you'll get the hang of it and you'll have a delicious and refreshing glass of water.

Serves one.

This recipe is brought to you exclusively by the Delia Telegraph

TUNNEL OF STAYING TOGETHER 'TIL THE KIDS GROW UP

THIS WEEK SEES THE LAUNCH OF GNOME DIGITAL

(DigiGnome)

giving you over **506** new channels and a wider choice of programmes to choose from — whether you like it or not. Not since the apple fell on Copernicus' head has there been such a revolution in communication technology.

Here are only a few of the epoch-making new channels for you to choose from:

● **Channel 94**

"UK G-nold". Restructuring of Channel 92's "golden oldies", classic movies including "They Flew to Bruges" (1974 re-make)

● **Channel 194**

Digital TV Channel. Order your digital TV equipment from the comfort of your armchair.

● **Channel 169**

The Paint Drying Channel. Round-the-clock display of your favourite paint drying action from around the world.

All these and hundreds more are now available for only a modest outlay of **£599.99**.

Full details on Gnometext (Channel 302).

JUNOR WINS FICTION PRIZE

by our Literary Staff **Lunchtime O'Bookz**

THE 1998 Booker Prize for Fiction has been won by a middle-aged woman who has previously been shortlisted on several occasions.

Penny Junor, 67, won the prize with her touching story of a fifty-year-old man who finds love and happiness after the tragic death of his wife. "Master Charlie", a historical novel, is based on a real life character and although she has done no research, Miss Junor reserves the right to exercise her imagination in order to earn a great deal of money *(surely 'discern the artistic truth of the situation'? Ed)*. Her previous novels "Prince Charles is Marvellous", "Hooray for Charles" and "Charlie is my Darling" all explored a similar

character and were described by critics at the time as "inspired fantasy", "classic fiction writing" and "tale telling of the first order".

Penny Dreadful

However, a disappointed fellow nominee, Lady Antonia Holden made a scene at the prize giving ceremony at the Guildhall.

An emotional Antonia, 75, attacked the judges, shouting: "I should have won the prize. She copied the whole story from my book. I made it all up first."

But the judges held firm to their decision, saying: "We can't all win, particularly not Prince Charles."

Camilla Parker Bowles is 107.

The New People's Poet Laureate

Now You Choose

TO SELECT the new Poet Laureate from the following candidates, simply phone Buckingham Palace on 0898 938 2424 and tell Her Majesty the Queen who she should appoint Britain's top rhymester.

POET	WHAT YOU WILL READ
Pam Ayres, Radio 2's Housewives' Choice	"I think I've got a touch of flu, Happy birthday, Charles to you"
Mohammed Al Fayed, grocer and philanthropist	"Happy fuggin' birthday to all of you at Court, Why don't you give me a fuggin' passport?"
Spike Milligan, millionaire prankster and Goon	"Ying-tong, ying-tong, diddle-i-po Prince Charles is a grovelling bastard, don't you know?"
Roger McGough, former member of Scaffold, the popular swinging group	"I wouldn't mind taking the job of Poet Laureate, I'd even write nice things about the Queen Mum's flowery hat"
Sir Elton John, legendary composer	"Happy birthday, your Majesty, You are a candle blowing in the wind on the cake"
Eric Cantona, poet and film star	"Les oiseaux de mer Chantent au dessus d'un bateau Pour votre anniversaire, Votre Majesté, un grand gateau"
Andrew Motion, Head of Creative Verse, University of East Neasden	"In Cirencester the nascent Thames flows calm, Happy 99th birthday to you, Ma'am"

FRENCH TEST
Boycott wins the Bashes

Lordes, Lundi

CAPTAIN G. Boycott led his all-women team out today having lost the previous test in France by an innings and £800,000.

New Coach Max Clifford said before the match: "Geoff is a good hitter and can knock anyone for six. This French judge should be no trouble, particularly as she is a woman. Oops."

Leg over wicket

Boycott opened the day choosing to go in to bat with his typical defence, ie: saying "She fell over" and sticking to the story until the lunch interval .

He was cheered on by the rest of the team, many of whom have partnered Boycott in various games in the past.

Mutton Dressed As Alan Lamb

Said one: "We love Geoff because once he's in, he stays there for a very long time." *That's enough filth Ed).*

LATE SCORE

Boycott seen in a bad light stopped play.

"…nice tits!"

OLDEST MAN IN SPACE

by Our Science Staff
Adam Mars-Mission

AN INCREDIBLY old man has been launched into the huge empty space opposite the Times editorial and is now floating freely on the page.

Lord Rees-Mogg (98), a veteran of space-filling missions in the sixties, seventies and eighties, has once again achieved zero gravity with a column about the devastating effect of Yo-Yos on the global climate.

Said mission controller, Peter Stothard, "Rees-Mogg has got the write stuff. He can write stuff till it comes out of his ears. And Rees-Mogg isn't just there because he is old. He has recently proved himself to be as unfit for the job as anyone else on the Times."

TAKE ME TO YOUR LEADER PAGE

Mogg himself is convinced that his attempt to conquer the inky void will prove worthwhile.

"I am carrying out vital experiments in space," he said, "such as how lightweight can I get without being sacked."

Lord Rees-Mogg is on another planet.

That Mandelson Apology In Full

Dear Peter

I cannot tell you how deeply ashamed I am about the unfortunate incident which took place yesterday evening. It was a quite appalling lapse of judgement on my part. I went to White City, as I have often done in the past, where I had a pre-arranged encounter with a gay man known only as Matthew Parris, the distinguished columnist of the Times. In the course of a private conversation on air, this man made an improper suggestion to which I foolishly responded, in the hope of gratifying my curiosity. I deeply regret the moment of weakness which inadvertently led me into the highly embarrassing and compromising situation — ie, allowing it to be publicly revealed that you are gay. In the light of the distressing attention which has been drawn to this regrettable moment of madness, I have no option but to stay on in my highly lucrative public position.

Yours Jeremy

JEREMY PAXMAN

P.S. Come off it, Mandelson! We all know you're one of them. You are, aren't you? Come on! Answer the question! I haven't got all night.

Late News

Birt Denies "Close Relationship" With Blandelson

In a statement issued late last night, the BBC Director-

General Sir John Birt denied that he had been involved in an "improper relationship" with the Corporation's Chairman Sir Christopher Blandelson.

The two men met late at night in a television studio in South London, but both deny that any impropriety occurred. (That's enough pieces about men meeting late at night. Ed.)

VILLAGE PEOPLE TO REFORM

♪ Go West (minster) ♪

Cabinet seating plan

So it goes gay, straight, gay, straight, gay…

THAT BIRT EDICT IN FULL

From the Office of the Dalek-General
To All BBC Personnel

Top Secret

It has been drawn to my attention that on last night's Newsnight programme, a most unfortunate reference was made to the private life of a well-known public figure. I wish to make it clear that this person's name must never be mentioned again in any context whatsoever, on any BBC broadcast, video tape, e-mail, inter-office facsimile transmission or digital on-line representation in any of the territories covered by the Charter, including Malawi, Puerto Rico, Rumbabwe (formerly British Rumbabaland), Vatican City and the planet Krypton. Any employee of the Corporation found to be in breach of this edict, DG/XXIV/7231/98, will be summoned before a Board of Management Disciplinary Hearing and exterminated. I, of course, realise that the issuing of this edict is, in itself, a major news item, which will inevitably make headlines all over the world. Staff are therefore perfectly at liberty to report my issuing of the edict on all news programmes, so long as no reference is made to the person to whom no reference may be made (see above).

Issued on behalf of the Dalek-General

by Ms Ann Sloperson

Supreme Political Advisor (Dalek Division)

DAVIES MEETING STILL UNEXPLAINED

by Our Man On Clapham Common
Lunchtime O'Cruise

MYSTERY last night continued to surround the meeting between the former Secretary of State for Wales and a man named only as "Tony".

It seems that Ron Davies drove his car to an address in south-west London where he spent three-quarters of an hour "in conversation" with "Tony".

They were then joined by another man called "Alastair".

No one knows precisely what happened next at the meeting between the three men, but it seems likely that Tony and Alastair suddenly became "aggressive" and the situation turned "very nasty".

COMING OUT OF THE CABINET

Davies was threatened, assaulted and then thrown into the street. Even his portfolio was removed, and he was left with nothing except his hopes of becoming the leader of the Welsh Assembly.

In a terse statement Mr Davies last night said "I am saying nothing, except that it was a serious error of judgement.

Everyone knows what happens when you go down to that part of London on your own. You're asking for trouble."

MURIEL! WHERE ARE MY BLOODY TIGHTS?

CROSS DRESSER

THAT IMAGINARY RON DAVIES MEAL IN BRIXTON

Menu in Full

Alastair Campbell's Soup

——— ✳ ———

Cottage Pie with Guardian Leaks in Piquant Sauce
Blackmail Pudding and Baked Genes
Coq-au-Van with Savoury Lies

——— ✳ ———

Welsh Rarebit (on the side)

——— ✳ ———

Spotted Dick
Bum Surprise
Resignation From Cabinet Pudding

——— ✳ ———

To drink
Camp Black Coffee

——— ✳ ———

Carriages Stolen at 2a.m.

Modern Nursery Rhymes

——— No. 94 ———

Taffy was a Welshman
Taffy was a liar
Taffy was a "known frequenter of homosexual haunts"
But Taffy was beaten by his father
Which explains everything

Anon

A Cab Driver Writes

Every week a well-known taxi driver is invited to comment on an issue of topical importance.

No.94 This week
Normo Tebbs
(Cab No. 4004 BC)

BLIMEY, guv. See that Welsh MP on Clapham Common? I don't go that far south myself — I turn my light off and say I'm going home. Anyway, bloody disgusting what they get up to. I wouldn't have one of them in my cab, let alone in the Cabinet. You can't trust 'em, see, it's like a secret society, the way they see each other alright, know what I mean? You scratch my backside, I'll scratch yours, ha ha ha. Know what we should do with those people? String 'em up, it's the only language they understand.

I had that Matthew Parris in the back of the cab once. A real gentleman. That'll be 58 quid, guv'nor. Traffic's terrible.

THE ALTERNATIVE VOICE

Cedric Spart, Co-Chair of the South London Society of Gay Druids

ER, the vicious victimisation by the Straight Establishment of an innocent gay politician who has committed no crime is proof, if proof were needed, that nothing whatever has changed in the homophobic police state that is the New Britain. It has come to a pretty pass when a so-called Labour government with a so-called liberalised agenda is prepared to discriminate against a member of its own Cabinet solely on the grounds of his chosen sexual orientation, ie by immediately sacking him on the pathetic pretext that he has resigned in shame, er...
(cont'd p. 94)

Anagram

Sir

In case it has escaped your notice: *Ron Davies MP = I'm no sad perv.*

Yours faithfully,
JEREMY PATTISON

Via e-mail.

Sign reads: "CLAPHAM COMMON TWINNED WITH THE MORAL HIGH GROUND"

HOW MANY MORE OF THEM ARE THERE?

■ EVERYONE is entitled to their private life, but the public also has a right to know about the nature of the men that they have elected to govern them.

That is why, following the extraordinary revelation that the Prime Minister and a number of his colleagues are active heterosexuals, the Gnome demands to know:

WHO ARE THE STRAIGHT MAFIA?

How many more ministers will be discovered walking around in public places with their wives and children? How many more accounts will we have to read of ministers taking their wives out for "dinner" in brightly lit venues during the early evening? How many more blackmailers will come forward with unpleasant stories of "hetero" relationships involving straight sex?

Come on, Mr Blair, tell us now who they are — or we'll find out and print their names anyway. "The truth will be outed."

PARLIAMENTARY DEBATES
(Han-z-z-z-ard)

House of Lords: European Elections (How To Stitch Up) Bill *(47th reading)*

Lord Mostyn of Williams: My Lords, I beg to move this very simple Bill, which is intended to preserve democracy by ensuring that all Labour candidates are chosen by my Rt Hon friend the Prime Minister.

Lord Cranberry of Sauce: I can think of no greater insult to the democratic tradition of this country than that people should become our legislators when they have not been chosen by the electorate.

(Tory cries of "What's the fella's name?", "Did you have the soup at luncheon?" and "Is Len Hutton still in?")

The Lord Chancellor, the Lord Lairg: My Lords, I beg leave to take off my historic trousers and replace them with something more in keeping with the modern world that is New Britain, to wit one hand-tailored pair of plus-fours designed by Augustus Pugin.

(Cries of "Get them off", "Have you no shame?" and "What about Mrs Dewar?")

Baroness Jay (Leader of the House): Is it not disgraceful that in this day and age people should sit in this chamber simply because of who their father was?

Lord Callaghas: Well said, Margaret. That's my girl! They should give you a peerage.

The Bishop of Neasden (Rt Rev. Jim Flannel): My Lords, I find it positively immoral that, at the end of the second Christian millennium, people should become legislators simply because they are appointed by the Prime Minister, as I was.

(Tory cries of "What do you make of this new chap Baldwin?")

Lord Jenkins of Bighead: My Lords, as something of an expert on constitutional pwocedures, may I wecommend that the discwedited system of first-pass-the-port should be weplaced acwoss the board by a wather more wational and democwatic pwocess, namely the single alternative transfewable decanter system, or first-pass-the-clawet...

(Bell sounds for vote. Lords wake up and rush through doors marked "Alive" and "Dead" into nearest bar)

The result of the vote was as follows:

For the Blair Stitch-Up Bill: 196
Against Abolition of Hereditary Peerage: 756
Pheasants killed: 3,512 brace
(plus one woodcock)

Speech bubbles: "THIS CLOSED LIST VOTING SYSTEM IS NOT DEMOCRACY!" "AND WE OUGHT TO KNOW! MY LORD!"

LATE NEWS
BBC LOSE TEST COVERAGE

THE BBC yesterday suffered another demoralising blow, following an announcement that the corporation had failed in its bid to secure exclusive rights to broadcast the test card.

Said a spokesman for the BBC, "This is a sad day for everyone here, as our association with the test card goes back a very long way. For as long as I can remember, the test card has been with the BBC — hopefully we can negotiate some kind of package whereby we get to show edited highlights of the day's on-screen action."

NEW-LOOK QUEEN Part 94

Speech bubble: "That Incie... bloody liability, isn't he?"

Happy Ever After...

A **Sylvie Krin** special from the Gatwick Collection by the author who brought you *Born To Be Queen*, *Heir of Sorrows* and *La Dame Aux Camillas*.

The story so far: Charles is celebrating his 50th birthday at Highgrove Castle, and Camilla is the hostess. She has been allowed to plan everything — but there is one thing that even she cannot plan. Will this be the night?

"**H**APPY darling?" "Er, yes, I suppose I am, sort of." The future King of England expertly swung his radiant partner in a perfectly executed arabesque, to the strains of the Band of the Gulfstream Guards playing a selection of the Spice Girls Greatest Hits.

No matter what the world was thinking, she had never been happier.

She caught sight of herself in an exquisite 17th century Jean de Florette rococo mirror.

How stunning she looked! Of course the décolleté ball gown by the great New York designer Agnes D'Eayton looked magnificent. As did the platinum and emerald earrings, borrowed from the Victoria and Albert Museum by kind permission of Heritage Secretary Chris Smith.

But it was really her own inner sense of irrepressible joy which bubbled up, like the Nettle and Avocado organic bath foam that Charles had given her on her 50th birthday some years previously.

Tonight, she was the belle of the ball! Of that there could be no doubt!

As the couple swirled round the glittering ballroom, Camilla outshone all the other women present. "Her" guests could only look on in admiration.

There was the Princess Carlsberga of Denmark, supposedly the most beautiful woman in all Scandinavia; and there was the golden-haired Grand Duchess Nigella von Budweiser, clutching the arm of her handsome fiancé, Ernst van der Groelsch, the heir to the Dutch banking fortune.

There also were the Hon. Tara Boomdeay, in her pink PVC trouser suit, only that week voted "Britain's sexiest aristo" by the readers of OK magazine. And there was the ever-young Lucinda Camberwell-Green, who had so often accompanied Charles on his tours of Norfolk churches. And next to her one of the world's former leading supermodels, the svelte Stella Artois.

How plain they all seemed tonight, compared to their hostess! What was it that Charles's old friend and mentor Sir Laurens van der Pump had written in his book *Gardening in the Kalahari*? "It is better to pluck the flower in full bloom, than to snip it in the bud."

Charles had underlined this passage when he had given her the book for her 52nd birthday, and had written in the margin, "How true that is, how very true."

THE cabaret seemed to be going on for hours, thought Camilla, as she looked at her 8-carat gold Geraldo Rattner watch, a present from Charles on her 53rd birthday.

It was nearly midnight, and still the moment she had been waiting for all evening had yet to arrive.

As she straightened his bow tie at the start of the evening, he had whispered "I'm quite nervous because I've got to say a few words at

the end of the evening. You will be there to hear me, won't you, darling?"

"If only this comedian would finish," she couldn't help confiding to the distinguished guest at her side, who had introduced himself to her as "Sir David Frost, super to see you."

The figure on stage was putting on a succession of funny voices, to the delight of the audience, who could scarce contain their mirth.

"I don't *believe* it," the comedian was saying, in a slightly camp Scottish accent.

"Isn't he brilliant," whispered Charles, "when he does his Trevor Macdonald?"

At last the applause died away, and Camilla was sure that her big moment had come.

As the waitresses from the trendy Covent Garden restaurant Mossibros served organic champagne, expectancy burgeoned in her breast like a thousand butterflies emerging from their long winter of hibernation.

A hush fell on the room, broken only by Lord Soames, demanding to know when the second sitting for dinner was due, as he was "still starving after all that nut cutlet rubbish".

Then the band struck up with the theme tune from Jeeves and Wooster, and Sir Stephen Fry, the famous celebrity, strode onto the stage dressed as Oscar Wilde.

"Hullo, my dears," he said, with a naughty twinkle in his eye. "I want you all to raise your asses — whoops, I mean glasses! — to our birthday boy, Champagne Charlie. Bottoms up!"

Nearby the distinguished statesman Sir Peter Mandelson, shifted uneasily in his seat.

Then everyone stood to drink the loyal toast, while the band eased into the familiar strains of "Happy Birthday".

"Speech, speech," cried the delighted com-pany, led by "Auntie Margaret" as she rose unsteadily to her feet.

"Come on, Charlesh, get on with it, so I can go out in the garden and have a fag."

THE lights dimmed, and Camilla felt her heart pounding. At last the moment had come when finally all her dreams would come true for all the world to see.

There was a roll of drums as her Prince walked over to take centre stage in the spotlight.

"Your Royal High-nesses, my Lords, Ladies and gentle-men," he began, reading from his notes. "I'd like to thank you all from the bottom of my heart for coming here today, tonight, for what is a very historic occasion in my life."

"There is one very important thing I need to say to you all," Camilla leaned forward in her seat. She could scarcely bear the tension. Was her whole life about to change forever?

"But before I do that," Charles continued, "I'd just like to say a word of thanks to all the good ladies who've worked so hard behind the scenes to make this evening the tremendous success it has been.

"And now for that important announcement. Would the owner of the dark-blue Daihatsu Land Cruiser, registration number SH26 BXY kindly remove it from the front of the gate, as it is blocking the caterers' van and they want to go home."

"Bugger the caterers," muttered Camilla through clenched teeth, as Crown Prince Haagen of Daasz hurried in embarrassment from the room, fumbling with his keys.

"What about me..."

BROWNNOSER THE THIRD

starring Rowan Atkinson
as *Rowan Brownnoser*
and
Prince Charles as *Baldgit*

Brownnoser: Truly, sire, I am about as sycophantic as the winner of the Annual Sycophantic Competition at Sycophants' College, Cambridge. *(Laughter)*

Baldgit: I have a cunning plan to make myself more popular by hob-nobbing with people from the television! *(More fawning laughter)*

Brownnoser: Brilliant idea, Your Majesty! *(Aside)* No one out-bottomkisses me in the princely posterior department.

Baldgit: Ying Tong Tiddle I-Po!

Brownnoser: Fantastic, Sire! Did you know that my nose is as brown as the brownest Brownie who is browned off *(continued in similar vein for several hours)*.

(Enter Rory Brownnose. Who else?)

Brownnose: My next impression is of a man who'd like to be seen as a dangerous topical satirist, but who really enjoys playing tennis with Tony Blair and going to parties with Prince Charles!

(Guests are carried out overcome with toadying hysteria)

"A little old to be in a pub, aren't you?"

PRINCESS PENNY'S TABLOID HELL

by Our Royal Staff
Lady Antonia Holden

PRINCESS Penny of Junor last night made a formal protest to the Press Complaints Committee over "the disgraceful intrusion of the press into her private life".

The Princess was in tears last night as she recounted how members of the Paparazzi had staked out her £1 million home, taken pictures of her walking her dog and even written nasty things about her.

"I couldn't believe it," she said. "I have done nothing to deserve this. I have led a blameless life being paid a fortune to write intrusive rubbish about the Royal Family. Why have they picked on me?"

Penny Whinger

Princess Penny inherited her title and her job from her father, the late King Jonah the First of Auchtermuchty.

However, the tabloids were unrepentant. Said David Yellow, Editor of the Daily Bum, "She is a public figure and a member of the Royal circle. The public have a right to know where and when she goes to the toilet."

SHOULD HE BE KING? Part 94

And how long have you been a basketball?

DAILY TELEGRAPH FRIDAY, DECEMBER 11, 1998

The Last Of The Cecils

THE dismissal of Lord Cranberry, the heir to the ancient Marquessate of Jelly, brings a sad end to 2000 years of British history. For centuries, the Cecil family has served this country with an unparalleled courage and distinction. The first Marquess played a key role in the setting up of the Star Chamber, which did so much to shape the evolution of British justice. In the 19th century, the 14th Duke was the leader of the so-called "Hatchet Set", named after his country seat Hatchet House, responsible for plotting the downfall of four successive prime ministers, including the unfortunate Lord Palmolive, who fell to his death while out shooting with the Marquess's son, the Earl of Loganberry ...razor-sharp minds... invaluable counsel... indispensable courtiers... obscure men in suits... totally untrustworthy... completely unscrupulous... this one worse than all the others... utter bastard... Hague quite right to sack him.

Tales of Merrie England
The Legend of Robinson Hood

IN those days there lived a man called Robinson Hood who took from the poor and gave to the rich — particularly himself.

And he lived with his longtime love Maid Millions in an agreeable Tuscan villa far away from the ghastly poverty stricken Sherwood Forest.

Then one day the Sheriff of Nottingham discovered some anomalies in the Paymaster General's tax returns and sent out a warrant for the arrest of Robin Everyone and all of his merry accountants.

The Men in Greed

When this news was heard abroad the Sheriff got a phone call from King Tony who told him to lay off, as Robin was "verily a good mate" and (cont. p. 94)

ROBINSON AT THE OPERA

It's not over until the fat cat resigns

TATE GALLERY PAINTING BY NUMBER TWOS

© Chris Offili-Bad

2 Dung   **2** Business   **2** Cak
2 Poo   **2** Doo-doo   **2** Turds
2 Crap   **2** Mess   *(That's enough shit, Ed)*

WHAT YOU WON'T READ IN THE NEW STATESMAN
(prop. G. Robinson)

Labour's Mr Sleaze — should he resign?
by Peter Wilby

Robinson — the unacceptable face of capitalism?
by a Man with a Beard

Christmas Books — How Robinson cooked them all

Geoffrey Grubbinson — don'tchahatehim?
by Cristina Odone

Disgusting cartoon of Robinson as a Giant Fat Cat defecating piles of money on a desert island
by Martin Rowson

Madame Bourgeois — a feminists' nightmare
by an Angry Woman

PLUS

Diary by Senior DTI official

26

TV

THE SOUTH BARG SHOW

Announcer: And now the 7000th edition of the South Barg Show, with presenter Lord Melvyn of Barg.

(Man with strange hair sits opposite bespectacled man in black polo neck)

Barg *(for it is he)*: Tonight we have an exclusive interview with the world's greatest living playwright, Harold Pinter.

(There is a long pause, followed by another)

Barg: Good evening, Harold. *(Long silence)* Do you think they're watching?

Pinter: *(Pause)* Who?

Barg: You know. Them. *(Pause)*

Pinter *(menacingly)*: Them?

Barg: It's getting late.

Pinter: Too late for them.

Barg: Yes. They've probably all turned off and gone to bed.

Pinter: Bastards.

ENDS

© Bargtrash Productions 1998.

THAT HONORARY DEGREE CITATION IN FULL

SALUTAMUS ANDREAS NEILLENSIS ALIAS BRILLUS PADDUS ILLUSTRIUS EDITORIS DOMENICUS TEMPUS SYCOPHANTISSIMUS RUPERTO MURDOCHI ET UGANDUS DISCUSSIONE EXPERTUS CUM MULTIBUS ASIATICI BAMBINIBUS IN PARTICULARE PAMELLO BORDELLO ET SUBSEQUENTER APPARRAVIT IN TELEVISIONE IN MEDIO NOCTE PORTANS BRACES RUBRES SED NUNC IN CALEDONIA RETURNAVIT UBI LABORET PRO FRATRIBUS BARCLAYI SINISTRISSIMI ET FAYEDENSIS FUGGINONUS AEGYPTUM CROOKORUM *(CONT'D. P. XCIV)*

©Napier University, Edinburgh

Public Swimming Pool Lanes

€ We Answer Your Questions On The Euro €

An Eye Guide To The Issue No One Is Talking About

Q. If we join the euro in 2002, is it true that we will have to pay VAT at 25 percent on children's shoes?

A. No, particularly if you don't have children — though there will be VAT on duty-free pyjamas, which are currently zero-rated.

Q. How many euros will I get for my pound when we join?

A. This will depend on a number of key economic variables, such as the dollar-yen parity, the broad-band fluctuation in euro-zone currencies between now and 31 December 2001, the effect of global warming and the next reappearance of the Leonid shower. Anyway, you won't have any pounds because they will all have been abolished.

Q. Will I be able to change my English euros for foreign euros?

A. If you are travelling in an EU country, your euros will be interchangeable at par anywhere within the 11-nation euro-zone, unless you are a football hooligan, when your money will be confiscated and used to repatriate you.

Q. Is it true that German tanks will soon be rolling down the Mall, and a swastika will be flying over Buckingham Palace?

A. The Sun says "Yes", and not before time. Wake up, Britain, before it is too late.

If you have any questions about the euro, please send them to the Eye, so that we don't have to make them up like the ones above.

"I don't believe this! They're standing outside having a smoke"

NEW CHRISTMAS CRAZE SWEEPS BRITAIN

by Phil Stocking

THIS is the toy that parents won't be buying this Christmas in their thousands.

Imported from the US, the FURGY is a cuddly red-headed doll that talks non-stop when financially squeezed.

Better Dead Than Redhead

This toy sensation of the season is primed with a vocabulary of up to three words — "Super", "Great" and "Wow".

But parent pressure groups are already worried that the FURGY could stunt the intellectual development of their children.

However, a spokesman for the manufacturers said, "If anyone is stupid enough to buy one of these, it won't make any difference."

"I think we might be busy — I'll just check the diary"

—PILBROW—

GLENDA SLAGG

* **Now you can download her from the Internet! on www.slaggoff.co.uk**

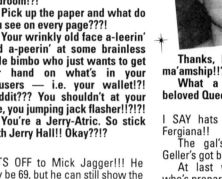

Thanks, but no thanks, your ma'amship!!?!

MICK JAGGER!!!! Aren'tcha sick of him??! Come off it grandad!?!!

At your age you should be looking after kids.

Not chasing them round your bedroom!?!

Pick up the paper and what do you see on every page???!

Your wrinkly old face a-leerin' and a-peerin' at some brainless little bimbo who just wants to get her hand on what's in your trousers — i.e. your wallet!?! Geddit??? You shouldn't at your age, you jumping jack flasher!!?!?!

You're a Jerry-Atric. So stick with Jerry Hall!! Okay??!?

HATS OFF to Mick Jagger!!! He may be 69, but he can still show the youngsters a thing or two about pulling the birds!?!?!

With his crinkly smile and gleaming false teeth, Grandad Mick is still the world's Number One little red rooster!?!?

No wonder there's a queue of luscious young babes stretching round the block, only too willing to give Mick some satisfaction!?!?

Geddit??? I'm sure he does, ten times a night.

And good luck to him!!?!?!

FERGIE!! Who does she think is?!?!

Her Majesty the Queen has bent over backwards to give the Duchess of Pork a cosy little £10 million, 80-bedroom house in Surrey.

And how does our ratfaced redhead reply??

What a way to treat our beloved Queen!!!

I SAY hats off to the Duchess Fergiana!!

The gal's got guts like Uri Geller's got bent spoons!?!?!

At last we've got someone who's prepared to tell those toffee-noses at the Palace "stuff your mansion — I just want to live in a tent".

Well said, your Fergyship!?!

They should give her a £10 million mansion in Surrey as a present from a grateful nation!!?!?

HERE they are, Glenda's Xmas mince guys!!! (Geddit?!?!?!)

Lord Cranborne, the sexiest Cecil since Parkinson!! If you want a second chamber, my bedroom's always got a vacancy!!?!?!

Sir Richard Greenbury! So you've got the sack!?!?! Bring it round to my place and we'll both jump in it!?!?

Oskar Lafontaine!! Crazy name, crazy kraut!! *(Surely 'guy'? Ed.)*

Byeeeeee!

TV CHRISTMAS FILMS

Christmas Holiday Monday

8.15am Eurosport **They Flew From Bruges:** Long-forgotten Ealing comedy where a group of West Country eccentrics declare independence from the European Union and set up the breakaway state of Euro-sceptia, under the leadership of Sir Herbert Gusset (Alistair Sim), Brigadier "Buffy" Frobisher (Wilfred Hyde-White) and the formidable Lady Gusset (Margaret Rutherford). Watch out for wonderful cameo from Stanley Holloway, as pub landlord Monty Balon.

New Year's Eve Tuesday

9.00pm Channel 5 **Titanic:** Made for TV re-make of 1998 classic, in which Emma Noble and James Major recreate the original Kate Winslet-Leonardo DiCaprio roles. Watch out for surprise happy ending as the ship fails to sink!

New Year's Day Holiday Wednesday

3.15am BBC2 **Gordon Brown's Schooldays:** Heartwarming 1933 b/w classic based on well-loved Victorian novel. Settle down once again for a good weep at the story of the young Scottish lad who can't add up. Starring the young Gordon Jackson as "Wee Brownie" and Joan Greenwood as his childhood sweetheart Sarah Macaulay.

New Year Bank Holiday Thursday

Channel 4: Long-awaited TV premiere of "the most successful British film of 1997" ***Four Funerals And A Murder***, in which a group of young unemployed Glaswegian heroin addicts gradually die of boredom while watching a new British film on television and then murder the producer.

"Brilliant" *Time Out.*

GENETICALLY ENGINEERED PETS

DOG JUST FOR CHRISTMAS GUARANTEED TO DIE BY JAN 1ST

RGJ

28

SHOCK LEGAL RULING

Murderer And Torturer To Be Sent Home

by Our Legal Staff **Joshua Rozenbeard**

IN A dramatic ruling last night the government decided that Britain's most controversial prisoner should be sent home immediately.

Human rights groups were shocked at the decision, but the Home Office said they had no option but to release the IRA General at once.

"We had to let him go," said a spokesman, "to establish the principle that no one who commits horrific crimes against civilians is immune from prosecution — unless they come from Northern Ireland."

BRIGHTON BOMBSHELL

Said the Irish Statesman's delighted supporters, "All these alleged crimes happened a long time ago, well before 1998 when the convention on letting out tourists was incorporated into British law.

"This is a great day for human rights, particularly the right to blow up other humans."

"It's amazing what he can do with Lego"

NEW-LOOK QUEEN Part 94

Put your coat on the bed... the drinks are in the kitchen

29

John Major, CH, for services to the Labour Party	Lord Knacker of the Yard, for services to Crime	Sir Fullswell Monty, for services to British Cinema	Nigel Luvvie, for being such a sweetie

New Year's People's Honours

(continued from page one)

PC (First Class)

Ms Judy Boxwallah, Chairwoman Women in Business, for services to Women in Business; Mr Raj Londis-Patel, Chairman Confederation of Asian Commerce, for services to Asian Commerce; Miss Fatima Wondulu (Bronze Medallist, Britain's Women's Sumo Team Commonwealth Games 1998), for services to Women's Sumo; Nigel Luvvie, for being such a sweetie (shurely shome mishtake)

PC (Regional)

Mr James "Jimmy" Shand, Scottish Musician, for services to being Scottish; Mr Thomas "Tom" Jones, Welsh singer, for services to being Welsh; Ms Garth Spart, Senior Partner Spart, Fenian and Witherspoon, Solicitors and Commissioners for Oaths, for services to the Republican Movement in Ireland.

MOT (Colonial)

Miss Evangelina Sheepshagga, Lollipop Lady, St Margaret's Primary School, Port Stanley; Christian Fletcher-Halfwit, Municipal Gravedigger Pitcairn Cemetery; Mr Alfonzo Baldwin, Chief Superintendent Ape Colony, Gibraltar; Miss Jemima Glendinning, Assistant Curator, The Napoleon Experience Museum, St Helena.

VICTORIAN ORDER RSVP

The Reverend Reginald Arthur Trumpington-Blewett, Senior Chaplain to the Queen Mother (Fridays); Sidney Warburton Greentrouser, Assistant Gardener, the Organic Conservatory, Highgrove; Lady Laetitia Featherstone-Limpett, Keeper of the Royal Beehives, Osborne House; Duncan Fraser McNugget, Chief Grouse Breeder, Balmoral Estate. *(That's enough People's Awards. Ed.)*

The Times

Popular Names

Sir, As is traditional at this time of year, I have compiled a list of the most popular boys' and girls' names in the year 1998.

Boys	Girls
Rupert	Elizabeth
Lachlan	Elizabeth
Rupert	Elizabeth
Rupert	Ruperta
Rupert	Elizabeth
Sky	Skyella
Jiang Zemin	Wendy Deng

This year, however, no fathers want to call their sons Christopher, Chris, or Patten.

Likewise, no mothers would dream of calling their daughters Anna or Mrs Murdoch.

Yours,

P. STODDART,
Duneditin,
Wapping.

Wedding Of The Century

How They Are Related

Frank Johnson	**Virginia Fraser**
Dr Samuel Johnson Lexicographer and contributor to "Ye Weeklie Spectator and Coffee House Gazette"	Lord Lovaduck of That Ilk 14th Laird of Lard and Chief of the Glenmorangie Clan
Dr Paul Johnson Editor "Ye Voyeur (incorporating Spanker's Weekly)"	Lord Fraser of Lovaduck 15th Bannock of Burn
Sir Boorish Johnson Columnist on Daily Hellograph	Lady Antonia Fraser World-famous wife of Dame Harold Pinter
Brian "Jonners" Johnson Editor of "Ye Wisden's Almanac (incorporating Cakes and Cakemen)	Lady Virginia Bottomley Famous wife of little-known MP Horatio Bottomley
Frank Bruno Editor at time of press of The Spectacularly Boring	Lady Virginia Water Well-known Home Counties golf club

---

The Eye's Exciting New Columnist!!

POLLY FILLER

THIS year I have decided once again to give up smoking. And I have decided that my partner Simon will as well. The first couple of days were murder and I nearly *did* murder Simon when he sneaked off for a quick fag under the guise of taking our two year old Charlie for a walk in the park.

Men — they're as much use as a dishwasher that packs up on Christmas Day! (See last week's column.)

And, to make matters worse, the Nanny came back all weepy and homesick after her father's funeral in Croatia — honestly, these girls are so selfish. Can't she see I've got enough on my plate looking after a pathetic, helpless, male baby, ie Simon, who has been in a foul mood because he's been staying up all night to watch the American Football on Sky TV without the benefit of his beloved fags. (As I remarked to a girlfriend recently, "fags" are what men are deep down anyway, let's face it.)

I lasted without a cigarette until Jan 6th, which wasn't bad going given how chaotic my life has been, what with the January Sales and the hoover bag needing changing. Dismal Simon, on the other hand, only made the first quarter of the Superbowl play-offs. Pathetic!

We have both, however, kept one resolution. We decided that the misery guts Nanny would have to give up smoking — or give up her job.

And so far she is doing very well indeed. It's all about will-power.

Happy New Year to all my readers.

Chapter 94
The Persecution of Peter Tatchell

OUR freedoms in this country have been hard-won. We think of such great martyrs to the cause of liberty as Wat Tyler, the Tolpuddle Six and Nelson Mandela.

But as the 20th century came to an end, another illustrious name was added to this glorious role of honour.

For years young Peter Tatchell, or "Pink Pete" as he was known, burned with outrage at the iniquities of the Established Church, which barred entry to the priesthood to practising homosexuals, except most of them.

Furthermore, difficult though it is to believe today, the all-powerful Archbishop of Canterbury, the feared and hated George Carey, had issued an edict actually refusing to allow same sex partners to be married in church.

Peter determined to overthrow these bastions of heartless prejudice.

He therefore set out from London, with a small band of followers, on a pilgrimage to the distant city of Canterbury.

THOUGHT FOR THE GAY

Here Carey was due to preach one of his infamous fire-and-brimstone sermons, calling on his congregation to try to be a bit nicer to each other, in a very real sense.

Just as he reached his climax, the gallant Peter climbed into the pulpit, holding a placard proclaiming "Death To Carey, The Homophobic Fascist".

He had barely time to shout "Carey, Carey, Carey, Out, Out, Out," when a mob of two churchwardens brutally asked him if he would mind keeping quiet because the congregation was trying to get some sleep.

Two years later the courageous "Pink Pete" was dragged before the courts and tried under an ancient mediaeval law which carried the terrifying penalty of a small fine.

In a day that will shame British justice for many centuries to come, a fiercely reactionary judge ordered Pete to be transported to an adjoining room, where he would have to hand over the then-astronomic sum of £18.60 (the equivalent of no less than 8 million euros in today's money).

The unfortunate Tatchell was led screaming from the court *(cont'd. p. 94)*

ABSOLUTE MURDER IN THE CATHEDRAL

A Tragedy In One Unnatural Act by T.S. Eliot

(Scene: The interior of Canterbury Cathedral. A service is in progress. The Archbishop is preaching to an attentive congregation [Sir Sydney and Lady Doris Bonker-Smythe])

Archbishop: I think, in a very real sense, we need to look at this word Easter more closely. We think of eggs, of chocolate rabbits, and of decorated bonnets in a parade.

(Enter Tatchell with four gay knights)

Tatchell: Who will rid me of this troublesome priest?

Four Men With Moustaches: We will, Peter. Leave it to us, love.

(The four gay knights assault the pulpit and push the helpless primate to the floor)

Chorus of Wailing Women: Woe, woe, woe. This will not look good in tomorrow's Daily Telegraph.

Curtain

HOW THE BIG STORY OF 1999 BROKE

by **Our Entire Staff**

AS 1999 dawns the whole country is interested in only one question, "Who leaked the top secret proofs of the book that Paul Routledge had written, but which was sent by mistake to the wrong address, or was it, and then ended up on the desk of the Editor of the Guardian or was it the Mirror?"

THE TIMETABLE OF DISASTER

It was at 4.37pm on December 21st that Peter Mandelson's top aide, Oofy Wegg-Prosser, received an anonymous phone call warning him that Charlie Whelan had tipped off the Daily Mirror that a fax had been sent to Geoffrey Robinson's office detailing a letter sent by Gordon Brown to Paul Routledge accusing him of leaking the contents of a confidential post-it note to *(continued on all pages)*

"Have you been going through my pockets again?"

SCOTSMAN IN SUIT TO GIVE UP JOB

by Our Political Staff
New Dawn Primarolo

A SCOTSMAN in a suit is to give up his job in Whitehall it was learned today.

The Scotsman gave no reason for his surprise decision, but said that he had done nothing wrong.

ON OTHER PAGES

THE BROTHERS

IT WASN'T ME!

ARGH!

ARGH!

A Spin Doctor writes

AS a spin doctor I am often asked, "Will you resign or do I have to sack you?" The simple answer is, "Yes, of course I'll resign, but you haven't heard the last of me, matey. I know where the bodies are buried you bastard you'll regret this" *(continued 2094)*

MIRROR

IS THIS THE MOST EVIL LETTER EVER WRITTEN?

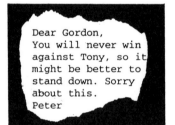

Dear Gordon,
You will never win against Tony, so it might be better to stand down. Sorry about this.
Peter

by Editor Piers Moron

THIS IS the treacherous note that Peter Mandelson viciously sent to Gordon Brown during the Labour leadership contest in 1994. No wonder that we now put it on the front page, so vile is its tone and so disgusting are its contents and *(cont. p. 94)*

MY FRIEND STALIN
by Robert Harris

I NEVER thought I would say that I feel ashamed to be a journalist. But the recent press treatment of my old friend Joe Stalin has been so grotesque, so brutal, so lacking in any compassion that I have been shocked to my core.

Uncle Joe, as he is affectionately known to my children, could not be more different from the man we have read about in countless newspaper profiles and biographies. They present a picture of a ruthless, cunning, manipulative, megalomaniac scarcely recognisable to those of us who know the real Stalin, a kindly old gentleman who is marvellous with children and who is the life and soul of any dinner party.

And what is Joe supposed to have done wrong to merit all the abuse heaped on his innocent head?

Sure, he made a few mistakes, but then who hasn't? Which one of us, given supreme power, would not act in exactly the same way as Stalin?

If the press carries on like this there will be no one left in politics with any talent, ability, charisma, flair or secret bank loans with dodgy businessmen (Surely shome mishtake? Ed.).

When I think of my friend Peter Stalinson, I see him sitting quietly in my orchard with his dogs at his feet, lovingly carving a wooden doll for his godson, Adolf *(continued p. 94)*

LATE NEWS

NEW JOB FOR MANDELSON?

THE ex-minister for Trade and Industry, Peter Mandelson, may take a new full-time job as Labour MP for Hartlepool, a position some have said won't suit his credentials as an ex-minister in the Blair cabinet.

Said a spokesman for Mandelson: "Someone said to Peter, 'Why don't you do the job you were elected to do and represent the interests of your constituents here in Hartlepool?'"

(Reuters)

AMAZING HOLMES. HOW DID YOU KNOW IT WAS HIM?

ELEMENTARY MY DEAR I SIMPLY BEAT HIM WITH A RUBBER HOSE UNTIL HE CONFESSED

FRAN

THE DAILY TELEGRAPH

Letters to the Editor

Damn you, England!

From Lady Carla Powell

Sir — Alla my life, I luvva the Inglaterra! Your cricket, your warm beer, your Englisha gentlemen like Jimmy Goldsmith!

But now I donta like you no more! Whadda you do to my friend Peter Mandelson, eh?

Now he's gotta no job, no money, no nothing!

He is a sweeta, kinda man who donta say "boo" to no goose!

I say whatsammatter you people? You gotta no respect? So shaddappa your face!

LADY CARLA POWELL
Bayswater Road
London

'I WON'T USE VETO UNLESS THE OTHERS AGREE'

Blair's New Get-Tough Pledge

by Our Brussels Staff **Eur O'Booze**

PRIME MINISTER Tony Blair last night hit out at himself for claims he had made last week that he would tell the French and the Germans where to get off over their plans for a European superstate.

"Whoever said that really should grow up," he sneered. "It is obvious that the only way for Britain to get its own way in Europe is to do what everyone else says."

He also lashed out at Tory leader William Hague for his "pathetic wait and see policy" over joining the euro.

"The only sensible policy," he said, "is to wait and see."

He then announced a £5 million government information campaign to educate the public on the benefits of joining the euro.

"We shall be giving both sides of the argument," he promised.

"On the one hand, we shall present the case for the single currency, and on the other, we shall be presenting the case against the lunatics, Fascists and Little-Englanders who don't agree with us."

"Try and be a bit more amusing, Agnes — what if Alan Bennett's eavesdropping?"

The Fables Of Lafontaine

No. 94 The Sun and The Wind – Which Is Stronger?

THERE was once an old German peasant whose name was Oskar.

And the Sun, the Star and the Mail had a wager to see who could make him the most upset.

First, the Sun came out and screamed, "You are the most dangerous man in all Europe."

Then the Star joined in. "You are worse than Hitler," it said.

Then it was the turn of the Mail. "Mad Kraut Oskar will put VAT on toddlers' shoes," it shouted

But Oskar took no notice, and went merrily whistling on his way.

MORAL: No one takes any notice of the tabloids, particularly Germans who can't speak English.

VIRGIN MAN'S HEROIC ATTEMPT FAILS

by Our Travel Correspondent
Norman Balloon

THE BRITISH traveller, Ken Punter, 56, yesterday gave up his third attempt to reach Manchester from Bournemouth by rail.

Ken set out last Monday on his record breaking bid with high hopes.

"It was my third attempt to make the journey and I was confident of being the first person ever to arrive anywhere on a Virgin train."

VIRGIN BUFFOON

But Ken was to be disappointed. At 11.43am on Thursday his wife received the following message by mobile phone:

"Hallo, darling. I'm still on the train. I'm just outside Reading and there are mechanical problems again. The train is being taken out of service. I just can't face it any more. I'm going to give up and take a cab home."

But later Ken Punter gave a press conference and refused to be downhearted.

"I shall try again," he told reporters from his Bournemouth semi-detached. "People say the Age of Adventure is dead, but I say you just try getting somewhere on a Virgin train."

Richard Branson is 58.

BROWN'S MESSAGE TO GERMANY

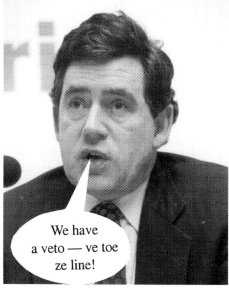

We have a veto — ve toe ze line!

TV Highlights

Shirley Valentine Cook

ROMANTIC comedy about a spurned wife of a Foreign Secretary who goes on a summer holiday to Ecuador and falls for the charms of a local guide. They enjoy a passionate affair in the steamy South American jungle, but at the end the audience is left wondering whether it was all just the older woman's dream...

Cast In Full

Margaret Cook . . . . . .PAULINE COLLINS
Robin Cook . . . . . . .NOEL EDMONDS
Don Casanova di Legovero . .TOM CONTI

Pre-School Nursery Facility Rhymes

Who killed Cocky Robin?
I, said Mrs Cook
With my little book...   *(Trad.)*

The Alternative Rocky Horror Service Book

No. 94 A Service Of Holy Matrimony For Persons Who Have Never Previously Met Each Other

The President Hi! And welcome to all
(for it is he): our listeners here on *(At this point he may say "Radio Neasden" or it may be "Good morning Fenland")* on 74.62 KFM, the station where news comes last. And a special welcome this morning to our celebrant the Rev. J. C. Flannel.

(At this point, the congregation may whoop and cheer)

Vicar: After the service we'll have the weather and traffic. But first, the marriage. And in the church this morning we have a lovely couple, N. and M. *(It may be Darren and Sandra, or it may be Dean and Lianne.)*
Now, all you two have to do is answer a few simple questions, and you'll win a free honeymoon in Thailand and a free canteen of cutlery for your dream kitchen when you come home.

Congregation: Oooh! *(Or they may say Aaah!)*

Vicar: Here we goeth. Do you, Tracy, know this man, Gareth?

Tracy: I do not.

Vicar: And do you, Liam, know this woman, Kelly-Sue?

Liam: I do not.

Vicar: Just one more question, and this one's for our studio congregation. If anyone here knows if these two people have ever met before, ye are to speak up now.

(The congregation will here remain silent)

Vicar: Great! That's it! I now pronounce you man and wife. We shall now sing hymn no. 94 'Getting To Know You' from *The King and I.*

THE READING

(The vicar will then read out the traffic and weather report. He may say, "There are long tailbacks on the M46 after a lorry hath shed its load", or he may say, "There will be scattered showers, clearing up towards the end of the afternoon")

Vicar: You may now kiss the bride. She's the one in the white dress next to you.

Congregation: Aaah! *(Or it may be Oooh!)*

Vicar: Well, that's all we've got time for. So, remember, what Radio Neasden hath joined together, let no man put asunder without first selling us the rights.

(There may then follow the divorce)

© *Radio Neasden, The Thailand Honeymoon Experience, Spoons 'R Us, Sheffield, and the Rocky Horror Service Book plc*

MEDIA WEDDING 'JUST A PR STUNT'

by Our Political Affairs Correspondent **Benjamin Wegg-Tosser**

A HIGH-PROFILE arranged marriage was denounced yesterday as a "sham" and the participants criticised as "pathetic publicity seekers who would do anything to get into the papers".

The couple, Tony Blair, 45, and Paddy Ashdown, 59, had little in common but were put together in "a marriage of convenience" in the hope that they would enjoy a "political honeymoon".

BLAND DATE

But the question remains — did they get into bed with each other or not? "No," say friends of Tony. "Yes," say confidantes of Paddy.

Whatever the truth, the marriage now looks as if it is over before it has even begun.

Tony has been revealed in the papers to be a "serial love-rat" who has had previous flings with both Margaret Thatcher and Lord Jenkins of Hillhead. He has also been accused of cheating on long-term partner Gordon Brown.

Paddy, on the other hand, has been branded "a glamorous airhead" who is only in it for the fame and *(cont. p. 94)*

A Doctor writes

BASTARD! Bastard! Bastard! Beardie Bastard! etc etc.

© *Dr Margaret Cook*

STORM GROWS OVER LEWINSKY BOOK

by Our Literary Staff **Bel Money**

THE publishing world was rocked to its foundation by news that a £600,000 book deal had been signed last night about the relationship of Monica Lewinsky and Andrew Morton, a man described as "obsessed by cheques".

The book will reveal how Lewinsky met with this man, the most powerful author in the free world, in a hotel room and immediately "had negotiations with him".

She apparently asked Morton to perform for her with a pen and paper. She then asked him to "simulate the writing act".

Moneyca Lewinsky

This Morton was prepared to do, and later he had several telephone conversations with her.

"I want you to talk filthy lucre," he is alleged to have said and the two of them discussed "oral cheques" at length.

Morton denied any "inappropriate relationship" with Miss Lewinsky.

"She made a number of advances to me, but I haven't cashed them yet. At no stage has actual 'banking' taken place."

"You've been lying again, Mr President"

WOMAN DEMANDS DNA TEST ON CLINTON 'CHILD'

by Our Washington Staff **AMBROSE EVANS-ABOVE**

THE MOTHER of an 18-year-old girl last night demanded that President Clinton take a DNA test to establish the paternity of her daughter.

"I want the whole world to know that the President is not the father of my child," said the woman, who would only give her name as Mrs Hillary Roddam Clinton.

"The idea that that lying, adulterous creep has got anything to do with my sweet little child is too terrible to even contemplate," said Mrs Clinton.

"Why can't the President just admit that we never had sex together?" she stormed, "And that he has no claim over my little Chelsea." *(Rutters)*

THE BAGHDAD BLITZ

That countdown to impeachment (*surely 'Armageddon'? Ed*)

Wednesday 9.24 p.m. President Clinton has routine Middle East security briefing.

10.04 p.m. President Clintstone informed that he will be impeached the following day.

10.05 p.m. President Clingon decides to attack Iraq.

10.11 p.m. President drops trousers *(surely 'bombs'? Ed)*.

10.32 p.m. Large missile lands in intern's mouth *(surely 'top-secret Iraqi chemical weapons facility'? Ed)*.

10.46 p.m. President successfully removes threat to world peace *(surely 'DNA stain on dress'? Ed)*.

10.53 p.m. Operation successful as President still in office (Saddam).

SADDAM SHOCK

He's a liar, he's dangerous and he's got to go

I thought you were on my side

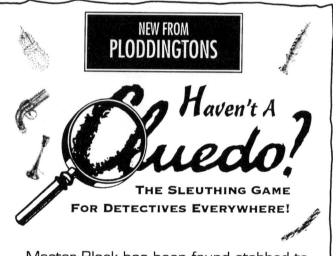

NURSERY TIMES

FRIDAY FEBRUARY 5 1999

'WE WERE NEVER MARRIED' — SINGER'S SHOCK CLAIM

by Our Celebrity Staff **Humpty Dumpster**

ONE of the nursery world's golden couples have split up amidst claims that their long-standing marriage was never legal.

The owl and the pussycat were married in an unconventional ceremony on a beach in the land where the bong trees grow.

The service was conducted by a turkey that lived on the hill and the best man was a local pig who provided a ring from his nose (the owl being notoriously mean and not having brought one of his own).

Jagger and the Beanstalk

But singing star the owl, famous for his hit ballad "O what a beautiful pussy you are", now says that his estranged partner, the pussycat, was never his wife and is not entitled to share in his fortune — estimated at a staggering jar of honey and plenty of money wrapped up in a five pound note.

The pussycat is adamant that the marriage was binding and her lawyers cite the wedding feast of quince and mince as clear evidence of the owl's intentions.

The owl has been linked in recent years with a string of girlfriends, including the Spoon's ex-wife, the Dish, and the woman who lives in a shoe who has issued a number of paternity suits against the owl.

Press Awards
BLAIR WINS "JOURNALIST OF YEAR" AWARD

by Our Media Correspondent **Sarah Shannon-Airport**

THE Prime Minister Tony Blair last night presented himself with the award for writing the greatest number of articles in newspapers in the last year.

Stepping up to receive the award, Mr Blair said he would in particular like to thank Mr Alistair Campbell for writing all the articles.

Mr Blair went on, "It is a difficult job being a journalist nowadays, especially in the political field."

TONY AWARD

"There is so much competition," he went on, "particularly from myself."

Mr Blair then read out a number of favourite pieces by himself, including "Why We Will Not Join The Euro" (the Sun), "Why Britain Must Join The Euro" (Der Telegraaf), "What My Third Way Really Means" (The Times), "Why I Love Geri From The Spice Girls" (the Daily Telegraph) and "Why The Stratoblaster Guitar Is The Most Important Contribution To Human Civilisation In The Past 2000 Years".

LAWSON ALLEGATIONS DENIED

by Our Espionage Staff **Lunchtime 007**

SENSATIONAL claims made in the House of Commons last night that Dominic Lawson, 43, is the Editor of the Sunday Telegraph were furiously denied last night by friends and colleagues.

"This is ludicrous," said one. "Are you seriously suggesting that Dominic goes into the newspaper and does some work? That's a damned lie."

Another commented, "Dominic Lawson could not possible lead a double life of the type you are suggesting. He has lunch all day at the Garrick and then goes home to the country. There is no way he could be an editor."

THE SPY THAT CAME IN FROM LUNCH

But yesterday MP Brian Sledgebore was sticking to his story.

"Conrad Black recruited Lawson when he was working at the Spectator. Lawson is highly skilled at chess and annoying people who work for him. He has a license to kill good stories and put in long pieces by himself."

Miss Moneypenny is Personal Finance Editor of the Sunday Telegraph.

"How are you getting on with your neighbours now?"

EXCLUSIVE TO ALL NEWSPAPERS
EX-HUSBAND OF WOMAN WHO USED TO BE ON TV IN TIFF WITH OTHER WOMAN WHO IS ON LOCAL RADIO

Full story: Pages 2, 3, 4, 5, 6, 8-10.

Thousands Die In Colombian Earthquake, p. 94.

37

TV PRODUCER TO MARRY PR GIRL

by Our Entire Staff

THE people of Britain were last night not in the least bit interested *(shurely 'over the moon'? Ed)* when it was announced that a man who produces television programmes is going to marry a woman who works in public relations.

From John O'Groats to Land's End, the story was the same — people turning to each other and saying, "I feel terrible with this 'flu. Have you had it yet?" *(Shurely 'Aren't they a lovely couple?' Ed.)*

FLU'S AT TEN

Champagne corks popped in the offices of newspapers, but nowhere else, as editors looked forward to a whole year of filling up acres of space with stories about "The Unknown PR Girl Who Is To Marry The Little-Known TV Executive".

That Wedding

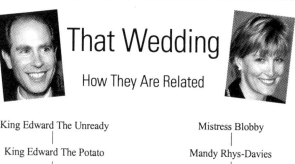

How They Are Related

King Edward The Unready	Mistress Blobby
King Edward The Potato	Mandy Rhys-Davies
King Eddie The Eagle	Mandy Rees-Mogg
King Edward VIII	Griff Rhys-Jones
King Edward Fox	Mel-inda Smith
Edward Bear	Melinda Messenger
Edward The Teamaker	**Jones The PR**

TINTIN ARRESTED FOR WAR CRIMES

Then   Now

by Our Legal Staff **Polly Tickly-Correkt**

AN ELDERLY Belgian man, formerly a boy reporter, was detained in Brussels last night and charged with being a Nazi sympathiser.

Tintin, 70, has furiously denied the allegations, pointing to his record as a liberator of slaves ("The Red Sea Sharks"), friend of minority groups ("Tintin in Tibet") and opponent of fascist dictators ("The Calculus Affair").

However, his accusers point out that during his early career in the Congo ("Tintin Au Congo") he supported imperialism and had a patronising attitude towards the native population.

His friendship with nuclear scientist and rocket designer Professor Calculus is cited as proof of his totalitarian leanings and calling his dog "Snowy" is pretty clear evidence of his racism.

Said a friend, Captain Haddock, 98, "Blistering Barnacles and Thundering Typhoons".

Other supporters include the Thompson Twins (Harry and Harold), who dismiss the charges as "nonsense".

"It was all a long time ago. Tintin should be allowed to enjoy his retirement in peace. Besides, he was only obeying Hergé."

● *Read Tintin's new adventure "Tintin Dans Le Prison", only in the Young Telegraph.*

NEW-LOOK QUEEN
Part 94: Edward's Wedding

BLAIR IN SECRET VISIT SHOCK

by Our Medical Staff
Spin Dr Alastair Campbell

THE PRIME Minister has made a secret visit to the front page of the Times, it was revealed yesterday.

Tony Blair decided to drop in on page one after allegations that the government was failing to tackle the NHS crisis.

Downing Street wanted to keep the visit quiet, insisting that it should only appear with a huge headline above the fold.

"Tony is not doing this as a publicity stunt," said a spokesman. "He really cares about newspapers and the chronic shortage of stories. He is doing everything he can to ensure that papers can be put to bed. Unlike NHS patients."

The visit, which lasted a good ten column inches, was a great success but there were critics.

Said one unimpressed newspaper worker, "If he really wanted to make a secret visit, why didn't he go to the Independent?"

"She's pressing charges — seems she burnt her lips on your porridge"

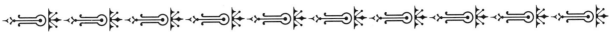

TORY RESIGNS IN SHAME

by Our Political Staff
Gay Search

A LEADING Tory Euro-MP has been forced to resign after admitting last night that he was "a practising Europhile".

Mr Tom Spencer confessed that he made regular trips to Brussels where he took part in sordid encounters with fellow Europhiles.

Mr Spencer told the Conservative Ethics Committee, "I have never made a secret of my European proclivities and I do not understand what all the fuss is about. I thought Conservatives were meant to be more tolerant to deviants nowadays."

Mr Spencer, who claims to have been targetted by Europhobes, was raided by Customs officers who found a stash of explicit pro-European literature concealed in a bag of cocaine.

Desert Island Discs

with TV's Sue Lawley

No. 94. Beethoven's Ode To Joy

SUE LEGGY writes: This tune is a big favourite with many of my castaways. It was written by the famous composer Beethoven, with words by the poet Göethe, who was the Andrew Lloyd-Webber of his time.

Posh Spice: I love classical music, and this is one of my agent's favourites. I always think of the European Cup which had it as the theme tune. Or was that the World Cup?

Damien Hirst: I first heard it when it was an advert for the Fujitsu Lagonda. Mega-brilliant.

Sir Edward Heath: I once conducted this famous piece in front of 400 million Chinese, who all said afterwards that it was the finest performance they had ever heard.

Taken from Your 100 Desert Island Top Tunes *by Sue Leggy, BBC Worldwide Money Publications, £29.99*

Tomorrow: Alexander Chancellor writes about his teeth, Sarah Sands has her hair cut, Tom Utley decides to carry on smoking and Editor Charles Moore accuses the Times of dumbing down.

"I've just turned forty"

LETTER TO THE EDITOR

The Disgraceful Example of Mr Spencer

Sir, I was disgusted to read in your 12 page exclusive that a Conservative MEP had been a purchaser of European Gay Porn.

What, may I ask, is wrong with Traditional British Gay Porn which is acknowledged to be some of the best quality Gay Porn in the world?

Yet, our industry is being flooded by inferior European imports produced in sweatshop conditions and without proper Health and Safety supervision.

Research shows that British customers prefer high quality home-grown British Porn and are quite prepared to pay extra for this privilege.

Mr Spencer has rightly paid the price for his unpatriotic behaviour. How could he act as he did when available to him in this country were such acknowledged classics of the genre as: *Boys From The Met, Meet The Marines, MCC Studs Take A Shower,* and *Ron Davies MP's Rough Trade Guide To Clapham..*

Yours sincerely,
MR ROWAN PELLING,
The British Gay Pornography Trade Association,
34 Filth Street (Top Buzzer)
Soho.

THE ALTERNATIVE VOICE

Cedric Spart, Co-Chair of the Tufnell Park Protect HIV Chimpanzees From The Bushmen Collective.

...it is totally sickening to witness once again the persecution of a totally innocent MP solely on the grounds that he is gay whilst pretending that he had in some way committed a crime by breaking the law about drugs and pornography... er, typically, the media have engaged in a sickening witch-hunt of the type that drummed Peter Mandelson out of office for a minor financial irregularity whereas his real crime was not admitting that he was gay along with 417 other MPs who pathetically resisted the legitimate demands of Peter Tatchell to drop the age of consent to a sensible 12 years old and er... *(cont. p. 94)*

MORE TV FAKES EXPOSED

by Our Media Staff
Daytime O'Booze

Y ET another guest on a TV chat show has been revealed as a fake today. A Mr Tony Blair, 42, has appeared on dozens of chat shows, including, most recently, the Richard and Judy Show on BBC1, giving his views on a number of controversial topics, such as the Glenn Hoddle affair and his wife's bathing costume.

But, it emerged last night that Tony Blair, who claimed to be a Prime Minister, was, in fact, an actor merely pretending to be a political leader for the purposes of the programme.

The researchers defended the booking of Blair, saying "We rang up a reputable agent, Mr Campbell of the Spin Talent Co, and he sent this bloke round. How were we to know he was a fraud?"

Said senior researcher, Ms Tania Daft, 17, "Everything Mr Blair said on the programme had been written for him in advance. He had memorised a script and was word perfect."

FAKE-TIME TV

However, critics who saw the broadcast said that the whole thing was obviously "concocted".

"You could see through Blair at once," said one critic. "He had no statesmanlike qualities and everything he said was clearly a lie."

But the list does not stop at Blair. Sky-TV was duped by eleven hopeless amateurs pretending to be the England Cricket Team.

Even when "the actors" lost by 176 runs, no one at Sky-TV twigged that they were not cricketers at all, but merely "punters having a bit of a laugh after a few beers".

LATE NEWS

The BBC has brought in veteran broadcaster Dame Enid Rantzid to head an inquiry into the scandal. Said Enid, "It is disgraceful for guests to try and make dishonest programmes. That's our job."

(BBC2) GREAT RAILWAY JOURNEYS

WILLIAM HAGUE
From Ilkley Moor to Baht-At

"You take the children's bath time too seriously, Norman..."

Announcer: Following the triumph of Michael Portillo's film of his journey across Spain from El Defeato to Conquestadore di Partido Conservativo, William Hague takes his own sentimental journey back to the land of his ancestors, Yorkshire.

(Shot of Grimthorpe Colliery Band playing Jerusalem in rain on rainswept station platform. Enter leader of Conservative Party in casual clothes — baseball cap, safari suit — munching Hovis fish paste sandwich)

Tannoy Announcement: We regret to announce that the 7.42 Great Northern Express Service from Ilkley Moor to Baht-At has been cancelled. This is due to the wrong kind of trains on the line (ie, none).

Hague: My grandfather was born in the middle of the Yorkshire Civil War. Half the county said that Len Hutton was t'greatest batsman ever seen. The other half supported t'great Herbie Sutcliffe. It split families down the middle. My Uncle Albert was a fanatical Sutcliffe-ite. While my Dad, a gentle idealist soft-drinks manufacturer, was a Hutton-ista. I tell you, many's the time they nearly came to blows on this one.

(Takes out onion and begins to weep as band plays "I Vow To Thee My County". Rain falls even harder)

Tannoy Announcement: There really is no point in customers waiting on this platform, since all services to everywhere have been cancelled.

Hague: When you've come from a divided background, like I have, you're filled with the desire to unite the country behind you and make Britain whole again — as whole as this wholemeal bread.

(Band plays New World Symphony from famous TV commercial. Hague begins to walk determinedly down railway track)

Hague: That's why I'm going on this journey. A journey to somewhere, from nowhere. It's not a glamorous journey in a fancy Spanish train, round places with high-falutin' foreign names, like some people's journeys I can think of. No, this is an English journey, Down-to-earth, Honest, No-nonsense. The sort of journey decent folk want to go on with me as their guide.
    So, come on then, climb aboard, even if there's no train. And we'll get there together, without the need for any blokes with foreign names and funny haircuts going on about how dignified and honourable they are, just because they're half Spanish. Who won the Battle of the Armada, I'd like to remind him!

(Brass band plays "Land of Hope and Tory" as caption "Vote Conservative" appears on screen and credits roll)

Tannoy Announcement: We regret to announce that this programme will not now be shown, owing to the wrong kind of presenter on the screen. Normal Portillo will be resumed as soon as possible.

EUREMBERG TRIAL COLLAPSES
Guilty men go free

So we're innocent then?

Damn! I've just swallowed my cyanide pill

'WE DO BELIEVE IN SANTER' EU's shock vote

by Our EU Staff **Brussel Twisk**

IN an amazing *volte-face*, the European Parliament last night decided that the much-loved figure of Santer was not a fraud after all.

Furious Euro-MPs had been claiming that Santer, best known for doling out millions of pounds worth of gifts to anyone who writes to him, was nothing more than a deception practised on the gullible by cynical commercial interests.

Santer, otherwise known as St Nickallyourmoney, and his team of "little helpyourselfers" have long been part of European folklore.

No one has challenged the story before now and it has been Christmas every day at the European Commission as "presents" were doled out to those whom Santer considered "had behaved themselves".

Suddenly people were openly claiming that they no longer believed in Santer and that they were going to close down his Brussels grotto.

However, common sense prevailed and the Parliament voted by 626 to nil to carry on pretending that Santer is genuine.

41

"Morning, Vicar"

Radio 4
Today:
Highlights

Sue McGhastly *(for it is she)*: and the really exciting news this morning is that there has been a terrible avalanche in France, which has killed a lot of people. Our reporter Sarah Hackette is in Chamonix. Sarah, as you look up the mountain, can you describe the scene?

Hackette: Well, it's snowing rather hard, so I can't see very...

McGhastly: You mean you can't see any limbs poking out of the snow?

Hackette: Well, no, I can't...

McGhastly: But surely you can see some arms or legs or bits of body half-buried in the killer drifts, that sort of thing?

Hackette: ...er, well, not really...

McGhastly: But wasn't there a story of some cable car crashing down into the path of the avalanche and exploding like a fireball, like in a film?

Hackette: Well, I wouldn't know because I've only just got here...

McGhoul: I'm afraid we seem to have lost Sarah there, but we'll return to her later when she's come up with something a bit juicier. And now, it's time for Thought For The Day with the Bishop of Neasden.

Bishop: Well, Sue, we're all thinking at this time about the terrible news of this avalanche. But, you know, the death of King Hussein, in the same week that genetically modified crops are uppermost in all our minds, makes us realise that, in a very real sense *(cont. 94Khz)*

Letters to the Editor
A King Remembered

SIR — May I be allowed to add a personal reminiscence of His Majesty King Hussein of Jordan or, as some of us remember him, 32067 Officer Cadet King Hussein? During the Sandhurst Passing Out Parade in 1923, I was standing next to the late King when we were inspected by a particularly ferocious Regimental Sergeant-Major, RSM Hastings (known affectionately to generations of "Sandies" simply as "Hitler"). Spotting the King's elaborate headgear, RSM Hastings shouted "Officer Cadet King Hussein, Sir! Take that tea-towel off your head, Your Majesty, Sir, and clean your dirty Arab boots with it, Sir!"

There was much hilarity in the mess that night, in which His Majesty was the first to join.

Field Marshall HORACE
FARQUHARSON-GUSSETT,
The Old Square, Bashing, Hants.

SIR — As someone who knew the Kingdom of Jordan in the happy days when it was the British Protectorate of Transjordanoland, may I add to the anecdotes which have appeared in your columns about the late King Hussein. Although I never knew him personally, I was privileged on one occasion to be admitted to the private tent of his great-grand-uncle, the late Prince Ibadullah. I handed him a letter of introduction personally signed by the British High Commissioner in Jerusalem Sir Roderick Massingberd. The Prince did me the honour of reading the letter, before asking me to leave the tent since he had some pressing business to attend to. This old-world courtesy was clearly inherited by subsequent scions of the family!

GEORGE ICHABOD,
former sales representative for the Anglo-Jordanian Electric Fire Co. (liquidated 1925).

SIR — A little known fact about the late King of Jordan was his enthusiasm for amateur radio. As a fellow "radio ham", I once inadvertently enjoyed the privilege of having a conversation with him over the airwaves. "Hello," I said, "this is Poached Egg from Hemel Hempstead calling." "Hullo, Poached Egg," I heard a beautifully-spoken voice reply. "This is His Majesty King Hussein of Jordan." "I'm very sorry, Your Majesty," I responded, "I was trying to contact Burnt Toast in the Solomon Islands." "Jolly good luck, old boy," was His Majesty's rejoinder, delivered with all the charm and courtesy we associate with that great Old Harrovian.

Yours ever,
poachedegg@newport.com.uk

Thousands of Foreigners Dead in Avalanche Horror

by Our Showbiz Staff John and Peter Snow

"DAHLING, we're all having a marvellous time!"

So spoke plucky English actress Patsy Pancake, who, along with 47 other British celebrities, has been stranded for the past 24 hours in the tiny, fashionable Austrian ski-resort of Unterschnee.

Talking last night on her mobile, Patsy described how she and her party had coped with the worst ever avalanches to have hit the Alps for over a million years.

"We're playing board games, lighting candles and drinking tinned soup. It's all tremendous fun, just like it must have been in the war."

No Business Like Snow Business

Among those sharing the white hell that is Unterschnee with Patsy are actor Simon Suave, socialite Tara Boomdeay and Fergie's merchant banker friend Henry Brocklebank-Brocklehurst, 22.

- Your Avalanches Tonight 7
- Dempster's Avalanche Diary 9
- Avalanche Horror – Blair's Message of Sympathy To Stranded Brits 11

EVENING LOW STANDARD

Julie Bullshit

■ GWYNETH PALTROW? Thyneth Paltrow I call her because she's disgustingly thin. And, like all thin women, she must be useless in bed. Men *really* hate thin women, and they much prefer big fat ones. That's the truth of it. Think of the really great sex symbols — Liz Taylor, Sophia Loren, Ava Gardner, Julie Burchill. They have all been enormously fat women who have written best-selling novels and *(cont. p. 94)*

LORD BADMAN
An Apology

IN COMMON with all other newspapers over the past 30 years, we may have given the impression that the late Lord Goodman was in some way a saintly figure who had devoted his life to the service of the nation and to philanthropic acts too numerous to mention. We may further have given the impression that he was a man of the utmost probity, totally scrupulous in all his business dealings, who had rightly won the admiration of all with whom he came in contact for his profound sense of honour, duty and rectitude.

We now recognise that there was not a jot, tittle, scintilla or vestige of truth in any of the above farrago of falsehoods. We accept unreservedly that Lord Badman was nothing more than a thief, swindler, crook and conman whose sharp practice with his clients' funds was matched only by his inordinate gluttony.

We would like to apologise to our readers for any distress that our misrepresentation of Lord Badman may inadvertently have given rise to. We have made a substantial donation to ourselves in full recompense for writing this apology.

© All newspapers

LETTERS TO THE EDITOR

From The Hon. David Astor and Others

Sir, We are deeply shocked at the cowardly way in which your newspaper chose to report that our friend Lord Goodman stole £1 million from one of his oldest and most valued clients. Such behaviour is particularly reprehensible in light of the fact that Arnold Goodperson is dead, and therefore is in no position to issue a writ for libel and a claim for damages.

Yours,
D. ASTOR
SIR EDWARD HEATH
MICHAEL FOOT
The late JENNIE LEE
The late HAROLD WILSON
LADY FORKBENDER
and all in 'D' Wing,
Ford Open Prison

INSTRUCTIONS:
1. LET OFF FOR A LAUGH
2. WAIT FOR FIRE
3. BURN

-PILBROW-

Student fire-extinguisher

THAT BLAIR TOUGH TV INTERVIEW IN FULL

Matthew Corbett *(for it is he)*: Sooty's got a question for you, Mr Blair, haven't you, Sooty?

(Sooty whispers in the Prime Minister's ear)

Blair: I'm glad you asked me that Sooty and, yes, I *am* doing a wonderful job running the country.

(Sooty whispers again in Blair's ear)

Blair: What's that Sooty?

William Hague is a laughable creep? You can't expect me to comment on that. Though you are entitled to your opinion. Ha ha ha!

Corbett: Oh no! Sooty's got his water pistol out.

Blair: Great! Let's export it to Sierra Leone.

(Enter Alastair Campbell)

Campbell: I think we'll edit that bit out.

ENDS

Olympic Round-Up
by Inspector Knacker of Scotland Metre

Six to watch

● **BACKHANDA** RUMBABWE's ace long-distance bung champion. Current holder of the Olympic Gold Watch *(donated by Salt Lake City)*.

● **EL BRIBO** BRAZILIAN national kick-back champion. Current holder of the Olympic Bronzed Model, Señorita Rita Legovia *(services donated by City of Barcelona)*.

● **FREEBINI** ITALY's internationally renowned payola star. Current holder of the Olympic Silver Cutlery Canteen *(donated by City of Sydney)*.

● **SWEETENA** THE bouncing Czech who currently holds the $200,000 record for Undercounter Payments *(donated by various cities since 1983)*.

● **HRH PRINCESS ANNE** *(Shurely shome mishtake? Ed.)*

THE RACE IS ON! LIB DEM TITANS BATTLE FOR PADDY'S TOP JOB

by Our Political Staff ROY HATTINRING

BRITAIN held its breath yesterday as the biggest power-battle in the history of modern politics got under way.

As veteran statesman Paddy Ashdown bows out, some of the brightest names in the Lib Dem political firmament were jostling for the supreme power that comes with the title "Leader of the Lib Dems".

PADDY SHOWDOWN

By late last night an astonishing 27 Lib Dem MPs had already let it be known that their names could be put forward for the most coveted post in Lib Dem political life.

They include:

● **Nick Cardigan**, 43, MP for Woolly North. Cardigan is on the right of centre, pro-European and believes passionately that he would be "the best man for the job".

● **James "Jim" Jersey**, 46. Jersey is to the left of right, pro-European and surprised his supporters by snatching the true-blue seat of Teacosy South at the 1997 election with a swing of 54 percent.

● **Jackie Muffler**, 41. Jackie is right of left, pro-European, and the front-running woman in the 27-horse race. Her constituents in Cuddly-on-Sea see her as "the man to lead the Lib Dems into the new Millennium".

● **Arran McSweater**, 69, MP for Ballaclarver. A middle-of-centre pro-European, McSweater is the former leader of the Fair Isle Council, who claims to have taken "community politics north of the border". He believes passionately in keeping warm during the long winter nights.

● **Nigel Kennedy**, 23. Boyish, intensely able left of left middle-of-the-road violinist, who hopes to take the Lib Dems to the top of the charts at the next election (Surely "third place as usual"? Ed.).

● **Tony Blair**, 45. Boyish, intensely able left, right and centre politician who, although he is not standing, is hotly tipped to be leader of all parties by the next election.

43

Lookalikes

Edward and Sophie　　**Bookends**

Sir,

　Has anyone else noticed the uncanny resemblance between the new Edward and Sophie stamp, and the cover photograph on Simon and Garfunkel's 1968 Bookends album? One of them, I seem to remember, was a successful couple who ended up hating each others' guts...

　　　　Yours,
　　　　MARK DAWSON,
St Clement, Jersey.

D'oh!　　**D'oh!**

Sir,

　Have any of your readers noticed the uncanny resemblance between the leader of Her Majesty's opposition and the head of that loveable dysfunctional family, Homer Simpson? I think we should be told!

　　　　Yours,
　　　　JANE DAVIES,
Biochemistry, University of Birmingham.

cula　　**Des**

ould Des Lynam be related to anybody?
　　　　Best wishes,
　　　　TONY GRAY
Lynn, Norfolk.

Owl

wonder if any of your readers have noticed the kable similarity between Keith Flint, front man band The Prodigy, and a tawny owl on heat? e they by any chance related?

　　　　Yours sincerely,
　　　　DANIEL FORD,
on SW12.

Cabinet Secretary　　**Ferengi**

Sir,

　While browsing the cabinet office website recently, I was struck by the resemblance between Sir Richard Wilson, Cabinet Secretary and the head of the Home Civil Service, and Quark, the Ferengi trader from Star Trek. Could they, by any chance, be a wholly-owned subsidiary of the Private Finance Initiative?

　　　　Yours,
　　　　A PUBLIC SERVANT,
Via e-mail.

Rusbridger　　**Potter**

Sir,

　Have any of your readers noticed the startling similarity between the fictional character Harry Potter and Alan Rusbridger, the editor of the Guardian. Could it be magic?
　　　　ENA B. ROWLING,
London.

Jeanne　　**Gaynor**

Sir,

　I came across this portrait of Robin Cook's new love, Gaynor Regan, on a visit to an art gallery. The sign said it was Jeanne Hébuterne by Amadeo Modigliani. Shurely shome mishtake?

　　　　Yours,
　　　　ENA B. PASTOR.

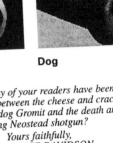
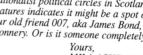

Gun　　**Dog**

Sir,

　I wonder if any of your readers have been struck by the similarity between the cheese and cracker-loving plasticine dog Gromit and the death and destruction-dealing Neostead shotgun?

　　　　Yours faithfully,
　　　　BRUCE DAVIDSON,
Swindon, Wilts.

Strasbourg parliament

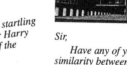
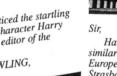

Huge folly

Sir,

　Have any of your readers noticed the uncanny similarity between the biblical Tower of Babel and the European parliament's empty new headquarters in Strasbourg? The new parliament cost £350m and will be used for a full 60 days a year — while, according to the Bible, the tower was just a huge folly.

　　　　Yours,
　　　　ARCHIE TECT.

Creature From　　**007**
The Black Lagoon

Sir,

　I understand a new face has appeared in nationalist political circles in Scotland. A study of his features indicates it might be a spot of infiltration by our old friend 007, aka James Bond, aka Sean Connery. Or is it someone completely different?

　　　　Yours,
　　　　MILA ASHENDEN,
Esher, Surrey.

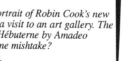

Robbie   **Kenny**

Sir,

Have any of your readers noticed the startling similarity between Kenny, the world famous singing star who dies every week in front of millions, and Robbie Williams, the world famous star of South Park who dies every week in front of millions? Are they by any chance related? I think we should be told.

Yours sincerely,
PATRICK BERGOT,

Crawley, West Sussex.

Mel   **Mo**

Sir,

Has anyone else noticed the remarkable resemblance between that talented, well built comedian Mr Mel Smith, and Mo Mowlam, the secretary of state for Northern Ireland? Perhaps they are related.

Yours faithfully,
DR PAUL MALE,

Blonde woman   **Blonde woman**

Sir,

Have any of your readers noticed the uncanny resemblance between the two blonde women who recently won prizes for their work in the cinema? One played Elizabeth and the other didn't... Or did she?

Yours,
BARRY NORMAL,

London W1.

Robin 'Potato Head' Page   **Jeremy 'Potato Head' Clarkson**

Sir,

Talking about Genetically Mollified Orgasms in the local the other night, strange evidence came to light concerning sinister and covert cloning in Buckinghamshire.

I enclose two recent newspaper pictures of Mr Potato Head — Are these clones? I think we should be told.

Yours sincerely,
RICHARD HIPKISS,
High Wycombe, Bucks.

Wyatt   **Lewinsky**

Sir,

I couldn't help noticing the resemblance between Monica Lewinsky, the Oval Office's oral assistant and Petronella Wyatt, the Spectator's right-wing orator and columnist.

Yours,
ENA B. SHANNON.

Roy   **Clarissa**

Sir,

While watching "Two Fat Ladies" I noticed a worrying similarity between Clarissa Dickson Wright and Roy Hattersley. Maybe Roy's dog mistook its master for the fat lady and caught the duck for Jennifer's banquet. We'll never know.

Yours faithfully,
JAMIE DAINTON,
Little Urswick, Cumbria.

Nero   **Boris**

Sir,

Have any of your readers noticed a resemblance between the great and good Emperor Nero, as pictured in bust form in the Daily Telegraph of 20 May 1999, and right-wing Daily Telegraph columnist Bore-us Johnson?

Are they by any chance related? And does Emperor Bore-us fiddle while huge piles of unsold Daily Torygraphs burn?

WILLIE MORRISON,
Inverness.

Hannibal   **Terrier**

Sir,

Some of your readers may care to note the startling similarity between the popular screen anti-hero and star of Silence of the Lambs Hannibal Lecter, as portrayed by Mr Anthony Hopkins, and Tammy, my mother's West Highland Terrier.

Not being overly familiar with young people's cinema, I presume Mr Lecter also suffers from a painful ear infection which tends to make him snap a little at his fellow creatures. I think we should be told and will notify you promptly of any impending sequel.

Yours sincerely,
ARNOLD VERRAL,

London E10.

Pinochet   **Calloway**

Sir,

Has anybody noticed the astonishing resemblance between once energetic band-leader Cab Calloway and his fascist doppelganger General Augusto Pinochet, the former Chilean dictator now resident in leafy Surrey?

Yours sincerely,
ENA B. McGEOCH,
Wantage, Oxfordshire.

Cook   **McEnery**

Sir,

Do any of your readers agree there is more than a passing resemblance between foreign secretary Robin Cook, photographed here in negotiations with the Serb leadership before the start of the bombing campaign, and accomplished Shakespearean actor John McEnery?

Yours,
BRIAN WARREN,

Maidstone, Kent.

YES, IT'S LONDON FASHIST WEEK!

by Our Style Correspondent James Brownshirt

ONCE again, London has proved it's the fashist capital of the world with a stunning display of young fashist talent!

And this year's look is already creating a sensation. Scruffy jeans topped with casual shirts (check or plain), all topped with matching de rigueur sunglasses.

As they swaggered down the sidewalk you could hear the "oohs" and "aahs" from the assembled reporters.

And then came the show-stopping finale. Dressed in dark blue serge with silver buttons and stylish pointed helmet, a group of young men proudly showed off the latest fashism from the streets. Produced by veteran design house the Metropolitan Police, this stunning collection was hailed by critics as "a disgrace to any civilised society" *(cont. p. 94)*

(cont. p. 94)

WE WILL END DISCRIMINATION
Knacker's Shock Pledge

by Our Man At Scotland Yard **PC World**

A REPENTANT Sir Paul Knacker today called for a greater degree of understanding towards minorities.

"The public needs to show much more awareness," said Sir Paul, "of those members of our society who are disadvantaged by belonging to one particular group, ie the police."

It's An Unfair Cop

"There is a stereotyped image of the average 'blue man'," he went on, "which is distorted and unfair."

Too many people, he said, think of the ordinary constable as:
● of low IQ
● prone to violence
● essentially dishonest
● connected to drug dealers
● likely to use weapons when confronted
● going round in groups, often late at night, looking for a fight
● driving high-performance cars recklessly through town centres.

Scotland Yardie

"No wonder," Sir Paul concluded, "that the blue community increasingly feel isolated from society, and driven to assert their identity by acts of anti-social behaviour, which only serves to reinforce their sense of alienation from the law-abiding majority."

Typical examples of hate-filled graffiti which Britain's blue population is forced to confront every day

*"We're not **all** racists — some of us are incompetent and corrupt"*

UGANDAN KILLERS
Knacker Flies In

By Our Man In Africa **Norman Entebbit**

INSPECTOR "Knacker of the Yard" Knacker arrived in Uganda today, at the personal invitation of President Musevenup, to solve the crime that has stunned the world.

Said Inspector Knacker "It is early days yet, but I have a number of promising leads. We are looking for 2 million suspects answering to the name of Hutu."

"I am personally convinced that the perpetrators of this crime are a bunch of darkies, as you would expect."

"My men and I are extremely experienced in dealing with this type of person, but the ordinary tourist should not in any circumstances have a go."

RACIAL MURDER

"If they see any coloured persons answering to the above description, acting in a suspicious manner in the jungle, they should contact our incident unit at Amin Hilton, Panga-Panga, Macheteville."

POLICE BEGIN EQUALITY TRAINING

46

LAWRENCE REPORT

We are all guilty

Except me — I was on holiday

The Eye's Exciting New Columnist!!

POLLY FILLER

As if looking after one animal isn't hard enough work (ie, the useless Simon, who is in a mood because Charlie put a jam sandwich in the video machine, thus wiping out his treasured Canadian Ice Hockey Highlights recording), now the toddler has decided he wants a cat.

I told him we're not having a cat because I'm allergic enough to dustmites without inviting a walking asthma attack into the house.

I tried to fob Charlie off with a goldfish, but the wretched thing died whilst we were all in Paris – apparently they need feeding, which the hopeless girl in the petshop might have mentioned if she hadn't been too busy serving people in the queue in front of me.

ANYWAY, Simon (temporarily roused from his beery slumber) then pitched in with the sort of thoughtless suggestion that men typically make – ie. one that creates more work for women.

"Let's get a dog," says Stupid. "Great," says Charlie. "And who is going to end up walking it at six o'clock every morning?" I asked, knowing the answer full well.

"The Au-Pair!" we all shouted in unison. The mutt arrives on Monday.

© All newspapers

NEASDEN WOMAN IN SHOCK CLINTON RAPE CLAIM

by What The Papers Say Investigative Reporter Of The Year
PHIL SPACE

A 68-YEAR-OLD Neasden woman claimed yesterday that she had not been raped by President Clinton in 1969.

Mrs X (Gladys Winterspoon) alleged that she had never met the President when he was a Rhodes scholar studying at nearby Oxford University.

"He did not drive down the M4 at three in the morning, break into my bedroom and have his way with me. This never happened."

But the White House was quick to deny Mrs Winterspoon's claims.

ORAL EVIDENCE

"We get a lot of these stories from women who fantasise that they have not been raped by the President. In fact, they usually have."

Last night Mrs Winterspoon demanded a four hour interview with TV's Jon Snow for a fee of £400,000 in order to give her side of the story.

Fay Weldon is 94.

TV Pick of the week

Princess Monica talks to Jon Snow

Channel 4

Snow: Your Highness, thank you for giving me the time.

Monica: Thank you for giving me the money.

Snow: Ha ha ha. Do you think President Clinton is constitutionally unfit to be head of the Church of England?

Monica: It's sad to have to say this, Mr Bashir, but he is a bastard.

Snow: I gather, Your Highness, that you suffer from an eating disorder.

Monica: I thought we weren't going to talk about the oral sex.

Snow: Ha ha ha ha ha ha. Do you think, Louise, that the media decided you were guilty even before the trial?

Monica: The President and I were very much in love. Or, at least, I was.

Snow: Ha ha ha. And I gather Andrew Morton has written a book about you called *Monica: Her True Story*?

Monica: It's £18.99 from all good bookstores.

Snow: How would you like to be remembered?

Monica: I'd like people to think of me as The Queen of Tarts.

Snow: Thank you very much indeed.

© Channel Four Hundred Thousand Pounds

"Spare the price of a cup of tea?"

GAY ROMAN GOBLET BOUGHT FOR £1.8 MILLION

Well, I'll be buggered

LATE NEWS
TINKY-WINKY OUTED

THE MUCH-loved TV entertainer, Mr Ned Tinky-Winky, has been declared "an obvious homosexual" by American religious groups.

The outing which has surprised no one is backed up by claims that Tinky-Winky's show "Loose Ends" constantly features camp guests with an unhealthy interest in musicals.

Also, the eagle-eyed fundamentalists have pointed to telltale signs in Tinky's autobiography, such as his admission to being gay and enjoying sexual liaisons with rough trade. *(Rutters)*

BLUE PETER STAR QUITS

by Our Showbiz Staff
John and Bart Simpson

THE popular BBC children's programme was stunned yesterday by the surprise departure of Cyril the Blue Peter Hamster who sensationally left the show last night.

Cyril, 2½, gave a press conference where he attacked BBC management for their attitude to the show. He said: "I wanted to cover, you know, really important issues like drugs and divorce and teenage pregnancy and stuff, but all they wanted was for me to run around my wheel."

RODENT RAGE

Said Cyril, "They're living in the past – today's kids want to see hamsters going clubbing and

Cyril: "Furious".

meeting popstars, not just eating corn husks and sleeping a lot. I mean, what's cool and nineties about that?"

Cyril's agent confirmed that the hamster was exploring other career possibilities, including total obscurity and cat food.

Blue Peter is 40, and good, so leave it alone.

John Humphreys *(for it is he)*: Clement Freud, you knew the late Derek Nimmo. Can you describe the kind of man he was?

Fraud: Derek was a most wonderful man. And a truly wonderful comic actor.

(Buzzer sounds)

Voice of Listener: Repetition of "wonderful".

Humbug: Over to Nicholas Parsons.

Parsons: I knew Derek very well. He was... er...

(Buzzer)

Voice of Listener: Hesitation.

Humbug: Well spotted. And Clement, that gives you 53 seconds left, still on the subject of Derek Nimmo.

Freud: I remember once when we were doing the show in Skegness, and we'd had a particularly good lunch with Kenneth Williams...

(Buzzer)

Voice of Listener: Deviation.

Humbug: Yes, I'll allow that. And, oh, the final whistle's blown.. *(Whistle blows)* ...So, that's it for Derek, and now it's over to Sue McGhastly for an update on the Kurdish crisis.

Sue McGaga: And in the studio to discuss the Kurdish problem we have Professor Norman Stone, the Reader of Modern Whiskey Labels at the University of Ankara, and the distinguished playright and wearer of black polo necks, Mr Harold Pinter.

Professor Stone, if I could come to you first...

Stoned *(for it is he)*: Bloody Kurds. Load of troublemakers, if you ask me, guv. Dancing round the streets, bangin' their drums, keeping honest Turkish folk awake. Know what I'd do with that Acalan? I'd string 'im up, which is what my Turkish friends are going to do with him anyway. I 'ad a bottle of whiskey in the back of the cab on the way here. Went down a treat.

(Very long menacing pause)

Pinter: ...You bastard!

McGaga: And now it's time for the weather. There are going to be scattered showers in Scotland, aren't there?

Weathergirl: That's right, Sue...

"We've been stuck behind this caravan for ages"

- PI4 BROW -

48

The New National Hard Core Curriculum

Devised by H.M. Chief Inspector For Schools MR CHRISTOPHER WOODLOUSE

1. Latin

Read the following passage carefully: "Inspector amavit puellam. Puella amavit inspectorem. Inspector et puella elopaverunt. Scandalum magnatum sequitur."

Do you think a) the inspector should resign? b) the inspector should deny the allegations? c) the prime minister should intervene on the Richard and Judy Show to call for him not to resign?

2. English Literature (Set text: *Lolita*)

In what way was it "educative" for the young sixth-form student Lolita to enjoy a relationship with her teacher Dr Humbert Woodhead? Think carefully before giving the wrong answer to this trick question.

3. Ancient History

"It was all a long time ago and I can't see what all the fuss is about."

Was this said by a) Alexander the Great; b) Plutarch; c) Dr Chris Woodhead?

(That's enough Corrh! Curriculum. Ed.)

"Smoking is against school rules, Miss Perkins"

OFSTED CLAIMS TEACHERS ARE 'INSTITUTIONALLY RAPIST'

THE SCHOOL Inspectorate, OFSTED, has today published a report attacking teachers for being "unwittingly rapist", particularly in their dealings with vulnerable groups such as white sixth-form girls. The report cites as proof of this the example of one particular former teacher, a Mr Chris *(cont. page 94)*.

'EURO IS TOTALLY SAFE' promises Blair
'I EAT IT EVERY DAY'

by Our Financial Staff G.M. O'Booze

PRIME Minister Tony Blair yesterday assured the British public that the euro posed no danger to the health of the nation.

"Our scientists have looked at this pretty carefully," he told MPs in an article in the Daily Telegraph written by Alistair Campbell, "and the product has already undergone the most rigorous testing in Europe for over two months."

YOU SAY TOMATO, I SAY FISH

"I personally would have no hesitation in giving it to my children," the Prime Minister pledged.

But Tory leader William Hague was quick to attack the government's position, calling for a moratorium for ten years until scientists have proved that there is no danger to British consumers.

NEW LABEL, NEW DANGER

However, a CBI spokesman Ablair Turner said, "It is too late to turn the clock back to the bad old days of the pound.

"Already millions of people are using the euro, even though they don't know it," he claimed. "The euro is already here, in supermarkets, in banks and in my imagination, and we should accept it as inevitable."

But consumer groups have made it clear that they wish to have a choice on whether to consume euros or not.

"We want money clearly labelled," said the Institute of Directors, "so that consumers know whether it is pounds or it is euros that they are getting in their salary cheque."

STOP PRESS

Man Turned Into Vegetable By Euro, Scientists Claim

A WEALTHY Henley pensioner today woke up to find that he had turned into a Labour supporter, after a lifetime as a normal, healthy Conservative.

Mr Michael Heseltine, 87, is believed to be the first victim of politically modified Brussels Sprouts.

Said his wife, "When he went to bed last night he was perfectly alright.

"But when Howard the butler took him his cup of tea this morning, he was sitting there gibbering about the euro and saying that Blair was a great national leader."

The Lion, The Witch & The [IKEA] Wardrobe

ARCHER'S SON FACES CITY PROBE

That's my boy!

Alexander Walker remembers Stanley Kubrick

I well remember the time when I visited Kubrick who was delighted to see me. "You're one of my favourite reviewers", he said. "You have changed the face of cinema criticism. I am delighted to meet such a legendary figure as yourself even though you are something of a recluse." It was then that Kubrick commissioned me to write a get well message to be used on a shot of a greetings card for a film he was planning but unfortunately was never made *(cont. p.94)*

Humphrey Burton remembers Lord Menuhin

I well remember the time when I first spoke to Lord Menuhin, or Yehudi as I came to know him, over the several minutes I spent on the phone trying to set up an interview with him for my book. He knew my work of course and admitted to being something of a fan. "I love your films," he said "and your books. You have inspired countless generations of musicians, artists and politicians. To think that your genius was recognised even as a five year old when you first wrote 'What I did in my holidays' (9/10) and were highly praised by Mrs Warburg" *(cont. p.94)*

OUTRAGE OVER SHOCK CHANNEL 4 PROGRAMME

by Our Media Staff **Gay Search**

THERE was fury last night after Channel 4 transmitted a two-hour programme containing no scenes of full frontal nudity, under-age homosexual sex or explicit bad language.

But last night controller Michael Jacksoff was unrepentant, and defended his decision to broadcast *Racing from Wincanton*. "This station is committed to radical television and we feel that this strand of programming has a vital place in the schedules. You and I may not find the sight of horses running around in circles very appealing, but a sizeable minority of viewers want to see this sort of thing."

HORSE PLAY

He continued, "We cannot have an entire channel devoted to homo-erotic pornography and titillating investigations into the British sex industry. That is just safe, boring and predictable. Every channel does that. Channel 4 must keep pushing back the boundaries of taste – and if that means *Racing From Wincanton* then that's fine with me!"

Channel 5 is even worse.

COURT CIRCULAR

BUENOS AIRES
His Royal Highness the Prince of Wales will attempt to dance the tango with Senorita Tequila Legova. He will be photographed by the world's press looking suitably ridiculous.

He will later address a dinner of the Anglo-Argentinian Friendship Association, at which he will outrage his hosts by suggesting that Britain and Argentina should "try to live together in sort of harmony thingie."

There will be a demonstration in his honour by Los Amigos de Malvinas who will burn Union Jacks and demand the execution of His Royal Highness.

PARIS
March 9: Her Royal Highness Camilla, the Mistress Royal, will attend a fashion show at the House of Tatte in aid of the Worldwide Fund for the Preservation of the Fox. Camilla will be snubbed by the designer, Stella McCartstudent, 17, and will wonder why.

LONDON
His Royal Highness Prince Philip will make a goodwill visit to "London's Theatreland." He will "go backstage" at the Raymond Revue Bar, Filth Street, where he will be photographed with members of the cast of "Just A Thong At Twilight", including Miss Titsi Slapper, Miss Jiggy Nicetime and Miss Rowana Pelling. The Duke will ask them "How much do you charge these days?"

WINDSOR
H.R.H The Prince Edward will receive a telephone call from Her Majesty the Queen asking him to strike off the Mistress Royal from the list of guests at his forthcoming nuptials to Ms Grifella Rhys-Jones, the public relations consultant.

"At last we're an item — on pages 1, 2, 3, 4, 5, 7, 9..."

YES! IT'S BROWN NOSE DAY!

by Our Entire Staff

TODAY is the day when journalists up and down the whole country cast aside their usual hard-heartedness and happily write sycophantically generous pieces about Gordon Brown.

Producing headlines like "Flash Gordon!", "Gordon Bless you" and "Vote New Labour", hacks are delighted to join in the nationwide celebrations of the Budget.

And there are endless ways to join in the "Brown-nosing"! Some reporters come up with pieces saying Gordon has produced the most redistributive Budget ever! Others say that he has produced a classic Conservative incentive to business!

But who cares how they do it, provided that at the end of the day the result is the same — millions and millions of pieces that will make "Brown Nose Day" the funniest day of the year!

YOUR AT-A-GLANCE GUIDE TO BUDGET '99

■ **Everyone in Britain will be better off as a result of Gordon Brown's giveaway budget, except for those who will be poorer.**

Check our easy-to-use interactive guide to see how your finances will be affected.

1 Man earning £11,412 a year, living with partner in central Solihull, non-smoker, with mortgage, no children, two rottweilers and small car.

Plus £0.35p a week

2 Unemployed single man, living on benefit in Bridgend, smoker with seven children, two unmarried mothers, drink problem and one small stolen car.

Minus £8,906 a year

3 Married man, earning £62,000 a year, living in Guildford with enormous mortgage, two children at university, one pony in paddock at back (Misty) and BMW parked in drive at front.

£5,812 a year better off

4 93-year-old widow, living alone in large house in Berkshire, no mortgage, two parrots and bicycle parked in hall (left by late husband in 1936).

No change

5 82-year-old former dictator, living with Mrs Pinochet in agreeable rented villa in Wentworth, Surrey, no mortgage, bullet-proof car and 79 lawyers to support.

£516,000 a year better off

6 48-year-old bachelor, who refuses to get married to long-time partner, living in Central London in rent-free government accommodation whilst working as Chancellor of the Exchequer, non-smoker, with large chauffeur-driven company car and index-linked pensions.

62% better off in opinion poll

BBC1

The Dyno-Rod Men

Major new BBC docudrama follows a crack team of drain operatives in Carshalton as they go round unblocking drains. This week trouble starts when Steve and Gary fall out over a backed-up U-bend.

Plus
Coming Soon

The Arsonists (ITV)
They come round and burn your home.

Upholsterers From Hell (BBC1)
Chilling fly-on-the-wall documentary, names and shames the worst upholsterers in the West Midlands. Horrific scenes as chairs are put back together with their springs hanging out.

Toad Rescue (C4)
The return of Britain's top toad rescuers with more pond dramas.

Lift Rage (BBC2)
Trouble starts when accountant Morris Fitzgibbon presses *(That's enough terrible programmes. Ed.)*

HOW TO COOK BOOKS

MIKE TURNER

"Do you have the one by Gordon Brown?"

RADIO HIGHLIGHTS: TALK RADIO

Smarmy & Nicey (played by Harry Enfield and Paul Whitehouse)

Nicey: Great Budget mate — very charitable.

Smarmy: Very charitable, mate.

Nicey: I love poor people.

Smarmy: I love poor people, too.

Nicey: We're very charitable mate — but we don't want to talk about it.

Smarmy: Talk about what mate?

Nicey: Er... being charitable to the poor and needy, mate.

Smarmy: That's right mate — we don't like to talk about being generous and charitable, unless we're talking about it on radio, television... *(interrupted)*

Nicey: Don't forget newspapers and magazines, mate.

Smarmy: Hey, I wanna word with you mate! Is that you keeping me and the missus girlfriend-type person up all night with that c-rraz-z-zy loud music and the... *(fades into business and finance news)*.

THE GUILTY MEN OF EUROPE

Your Cut-Out-And-Keep-Guide To Those European Commissioners They Had To Sack

Klaus Handintill, 52, former Deputy Leader of the Bavarian Social Christian Party. Has been Commissioner for Organic Olives And Media Studies since 1996. The report described him as "a bit shifty but totally innocent".

Emma La Payola, 46, former Chief Advisor to the Spanish Government on contraception policy. Has been Commissioner for School Milk, Airports and Bull-fighting since 1996. The report acquits her of any wrongdoing, apart from being "a bit dodgy".

Herge Bribe, 48, former Mayor of Bruges. Has been Commissioner for Tax Harmonisation, Sandwiches and Underfloor Heating since 1995. The report could find no fault with his thoroughly suspicious conduct.

Sir Leon Brittan, 58, formerly failed British politician. Has been Commissioner for External Lunches, Trading Stamps and Non-Spanish Omelettes since 1988. The report found Sir Leon to be "an innocent slimy creep".

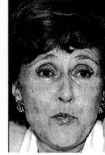

Madame Eugenie Croissant, 57, former mistress of the President of France. Commissioner for Fraud, Mismanagement and Sado-Nepotism since 1997. The report found her to be "totally corrupt and a suitable scapegoat for all the other innocent Commissioners."

Santer Klaus, 62, formerly President of Radio Luxemburg. President of the European Commission since 1994, responsible for Doing Nothing And Getting Away With It. The report totally exonerated him, but recommended that he should "resign immediately before they find out what he's been up to".

(That's enough innocent guilty men. Ed.)

WHO ARE THEY — The New Whiter-Than-White EC Commissioners Who Will Take Europe Into The New Sleaze-Free Millennium?

See above with a few exceptions to make it look as though things have changed.

Letters to the Editor

Lord Denning Remembered

Sir—I once had the inestimable privilege of appearing before Tom Denning when he was in the Chancery and Probate division of the High Court. The case concerned the will of a wealthy pig farmer who had bequested one of his prize sows to his housekeeper, a Mrs. Elsworthy if I remember correctly, who had also died. My final submission, thanks to the complexity of the case, unavoidably lasted several weeks. I was still in mid-flow, when Lord Denning, with his typical old-world courtesy and charm, interrupted me in his gentle Hampshire burr and suggested that I should "shut up and sit down". What a wise old gentleman he was! We shall not see his like again.

SIR ARCHIBALD HUGEFEE Q.C.
The Inner Temple.

Sir—The people of Wittering St. Parva will be extremely grateful to the late Lord Denning for the preservation of the ancient footpath which for centuries has run from their village to the neighbouring village of Fearnley Whittingstall. When the path was threatened with closure in 1918, it was the already venerable Lord Denning who wrote to the Clerk of the Parish Council in his own inimitable handwriting, warning them that if they dared to allow the closure of the said footpath, he would personally take pleasure in sentencing them all to death. As he himself put it, citing the great 17th Century jurist Jefferies J., "be ye whomsoever ye may be, be ye so high, or be ye so low, I am above ye and ye shall be strung up, for it is ye only language that ye understand."

MRS CYNTHIA VOLECLAMP
The Old Kissing Gate
Boris St Johnson
Dorset

Sir—Tom Denning was the greatest judge in British history, as I have good reason to know. Whereas most judges sent me down for a couple of weeks at most, or even let me off altogether, Lord Denning could not be taken in by the likes of me. When I was found guilty of shoplifting a packet of Wood-bines from a Neasden tobacco-nist, he quite rightly sentenced me to 35 years hard labour. "I can see you are a foreigner" he said in his funny Hampshire voice. "We don't want your type coming over here and stealing our cigarettes. You shall be taken from this place and hanged by the neck. Be ye never so alive, you shall soon be dead, praise be to God, for it is the only language you darkies understand."

REGINALD CARRUTHERS
Dartmoor Prison

Sir—I wish to protest at the suggestion in the above letter that Lord Denning was an institutional racist. This is a most vile and tasteless slur on a man who is no longer alive to defend himself. Lord Denning came from another era, when there were few black people in England, thank goodness.

E. MOSLEY POWELL
Foaming-on-the-Tiber
Warwicks

LORD DENNING IS DEAD !

HE'LL HAVE TO *RETIRE* SOON !

M.P. FOUND IN HOUSE OF COMMONS

by Our Political Staff **Huge Montgomery-Massagebird**

A SENIOR labour figure was discovered last night in a seedy Westminster establishment frequented by low-life men and women imported from the MIdlands to massage Tony Blair's ego.

Said the unnamed M.P. Joe Ashton "Yes I was there. I see nothing wrong in that. It is perfectly legal to attend the House of Commons, particularly as they have late sessions."

HANDSARD JOB

He continued, "After a stressful day in the massage parlour you can lie on a nice leather bench and relax. The speeches just wash over you and the soothing hot air soon takes all your cares away."

Joe Ashton is 69

"At least he's on massage!"

TV QUIZ SHOW RIGGED
More Shock Revelations

Y ET ANOTHER popular TV panel game has been exposed as "a complete fraud".

It has been revealed that contestants in the weekly show 'Prime Minister's Question Time' are not only given advance warning of the questions but they are fed the answers by teams of experts behind the scenes.

Just a 30 Minutes

In a typical recent exchange between the two team leaders, William Hague asked Tony Blair:

by Our Showbiz Staff Matthew Parris-Studio

"Would the right honourable gentleman tell us precisely how much taxes have been increased since he came to power?"

Quick as a flash, Tony Blair quipped: "I think you'll find that we won the election, not you, you little squit!"

Clearly both question and answer were prepared beforehand, though viewers were led to believe that this was an example of spontaneous parliamentary wit at its finest.

NEW-LOOK QUEEN MOTHER
No. 94: Trouble with the Bookies

You better find the money from somewhere, Mum, or they'll come round and break yer legs

RED NOSE DAY SPECIAL

SNORTING WITH LAUGHTER!

BBC1 Thursday 9.30pm

A team of top comics and celebrities travel to Third World Colombia to find out for themselves how appalling conditions are for the region's cocaine growers. They discover that the simple coke farmers need lots of Western money just to keep going. Without that money they will not be able to grow the top quality narcotics that the TV celebrities have grown to expect. Nor will they be able to buy vital equipment to maintain their livelihoods — such as helicopter gunships, anti-personnel mines and AK47s.

Western governments, led by America, are deliberately trying to withhold the money which the one crop economy badly needs.

But now with the help of the Red Itchy, Sore, Nose team of top TV and film personalities these humble cartel barons can now look forward to a secure future plying their centuries-old trade to the comedy and acting professions of the First World.

● **Buy the hit single**
"There won't be snow in the Groucho Club at Christmas"

Radio And TV Highlights

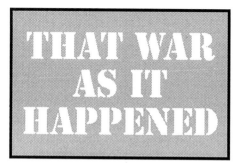

THAT WAR AS IT HAPPENED

What You Missed

Day Two

Phil Airtime (Presenter): And the latest news coming out of Belgrade is that things are pretty confused. But for an up-to-the-minute report on what is happening there, we go over to Olga Volga in Belgrade.

(Still photo of hackette in flakette jackette)

Olga *(for it is she)*: That's right, Phil. The situation here in Belgrade really is pretty confused. We're locked in our hotel room, so we can't really find out very much, but I think I did see a flash outside the window an hour ago.

Phil: Was that a pretty big flash, Olga?

Olga: Well, it was hard to tell. It was either a very big flash a long way away, or possibly a rather small flash a good deal nearer.

Sue McGhastly *(for it is she)*: Olga, could you see any Serb bodies flying through the air, women and children, that kind of thing?

Phil: You're on the wrong station, Sue.

Sue: Sorry, back over to Olga. What is the mood amongst the ordinary Serbs?

Olga: Well, it's very hard to tell at this stage, because we're stuck here on the 15th floor of our hotel, and from this height the mood is quite difficult to gauge. Also, there's nothing on the television, which means we have no first-hand knowledge of how people are feeling.

Phil: Have you got John Simpson, the BBC's Supreme Global Affairs Editor, with you?

John Simpson *(for it is he)*: The situation is very serious indeed. In fact, in all my years of reporting on major world crises, I cannot remember any situation quite as perilous as the one which is now confronting us. Only five minutes ago the Serb police ordered me to hand over my mobile phone.

Phil: That sounds terrible, John. Our thoughts are with you. And we'll come back for an update just as soon as we've run out of guests in the studio. And later in the programme we'll be talking to Tony Blair, Robin Cook, Paddy Ashdown, George Robertson, Madeleine Albright, Kofi Annan, Sir Peter de la Billiere and Tony Benn, just as soon as they've finished on Sky News. But first we go over to Bob Waffle at RAF Fairford. Bob, what's happening down there? Is it pretty dramatic?

Bob: That's right, Phil. Things are pretty quiet here. In fact, from where I am, I can see a barbed wire fence, a few trees and an empty airfield. But tonight it'll all look very different. I won't be able to see anything at all because it will be dark.

Phil: So, what's the mood like amongst our boys, Bob?

Bob: Morale is very high, Phil. All the journalists I've spoken to are feeling pretty confident. They've got a job to do, and they're going out there to do it.

Phil: I meant the pilots, Bob.

Bob: I haven't seen any of those, Phil. But tonight it will be very different.

Phil: Thank you, Bob. And to discuss that dramatic report, here in the studio we have Air Vice-Commodore Sir John Prang-Throttle, former Deputy Head of the Defence Intelligence Staff during Operation Desert Song. Sir John, could I come to you first, since you're the only person here? How effective do you think this bombing can be?

Sir John: Well, that very much depends on how effective the bombing is. And that will depend on a number of factors. Firstly, bombing effectiveness. Secondly, the effectiveness of the bombing. And thirdly...

Phil: I'm afraid I'm going to cut you short

Something happening, somewhere

there, Sir John, because we've got a report just coming in from the Yugoslavian Embassy, where we have the Yugoslav Deputy Assistant Attaché Slobodan Rubbergluv. Mr Rubbergluv, how do you react to the bombing? Do you think it's a good idea, or a bad idea?

Rubbergluv: You are all bastards. We Serbs will not be intimidated by international gangsterism. Excuse me, I must now go to shelter.

Phil: Thank you very much. And now, for the background to the conflict, we've got Professor Sir Herbert Sherbert, reader in Serb History at the Institute of Sherbo-Croatian Studies. Professor, I gather that the whole thing really goes back to 1292. Is that right?

Professor: Yes, that's right, Phil. It is impossible to understand why the Americans are bombing Kosovo in 1999, without knowing about the last stand of Prince Gazza the Great against the armed might of the Ottoman Emperor Saladbar the Incomparable at the Battle of Natov. It was this historic defeat which in 1323 led to...

Phil: I'm afraid I'm going to have to cut you off there because we've got a very important update on what is happening in Belgrade. John Simpson, I gather there have been dramatic developments even in the last few minutes?

Simpson: Yes, Phil, I've spoken to the hotel porter, and he tells me that breakfast is going to be a little late because of some sort of bombing that's going on. But I can tell you that the mood is
(cont'd 94 KHz)

Letters to the Editor

War In The Balkans

SIR—For those who understand the history of the Balkans, the current NATO strategy looks increasingly pathetic.

Don't these people realise that the Macedonians are a proud island race, all personally descended from Alexander the Hun. No wonder these gallant warriors of the Steppes have for centuries fought off the advances of the Islamic hordes from neighbouring Albinonia.

Surely this is time for we Christians to stand shoulder to shoulder with our Serb brothers, by remaining neutral and leaving all these ghastly little people who live in the Balkans alone to kill each other in peace.

ALAN CLARK MP
Serbwood Castle

SIR—Of course we're all frightfully sympathetic to the plight of the millions of refugees whom we see on our television night after night, when we are not out to dinner with our friends. But, frankly, what could be more absurd than the idea that we in this tiny little island should be forced to admit thousands of these primitive peasants to Britain, no doubt to sponge off our welfare state like those awful Kurds. Surely the country to which all these refugees should be sent is America, which has plenty of suitable places to put them, eg the Grand Canyon. Anyway, it's all Mr Clinton's fault that we've got into this mess, and it should now be up to him to sort it all out.

Lady OLGA BOATMAN
Ephraim St Hardcastle, Berks

SIR—No one can hope to understand the present situation in the Balkans without an intimate knowledge of the recent history of this troubled region. In 1943 I was parachuted into central Kosovonia (now Kosovenia) to assist the Croat partisans under Jan Fascisto, the leader of the PQVD Militia, in their advance over the River Murda to attack the Royalist Serb partisans, led by General Mikhail Nazivich, who were at that time assisting the Wehrmacht in their attempt to subdue the beleaguered Bosno-Hertzarentakar enclave occupied by the Albano-Montenegro Chetniks under Col. Vlad Impala. To cut a long story short, I was immediately arrested and took no further part in the war. However, my experiences there led me to a firm conviction that it is very foolish to underestimate the fighting capabilities of Johnny Serb, especially when his anger has been roused.

Sir FITZROY MACLOON
(Dec'd)
Tiko Towers, Ayrshire

SIR—Nothing about this war has shocked me more than the sight of a minister of the British Crown, Mrs Clare Short, arriving in Macedonia in a pair of patent leather shoes. Such discourtesy to her Macedonian hosts was truly unforgiveable. Surely a pair of stout Wellington boots should have been included in her luggage by her civil servants. Truly, it can be said that Whitehall was unprepared for this so-called catastrophe.

Lady PRISTINA BROWN
Killycroat, County Clareshort, Eire

SIR—No one seems to have thought through the implications of allowing the displaced Kosovans to settle in neighbouring countries. For example, the ethnic mix in Macemurdia is currently finely balanced at 27.3 percent Serbs; 31.4 percent Muslims; and 32.7 percent journalists trying to interview the above. Any further influx of minority populations could well create a domino effect, leading to intervention by the Bulgaro-Albranians, the Greco-Hungarians and the Slovenio-Moldovans, and all the other ethnic minorities who comprise what Bismark described as "Europe's hot potato waiting to turn into a tidal wave". We, like he, should know when to leave well alone.

Prof Sir B. O'CROAT
Institute of Balkanological Studies
University of Tiranamisu

SIR—As an independent commentator who holds no brief for either the drug-peddling Marxists of the KLA or the warmongering Fascists of NATO, I am shocked at the way the slavish British media are ignoring the tragic plight of thousands of Serbs, who have been forced from their homes to go into Kosovo and murder everybody. And what of the much-maligned St Slobodan of Milosevic, whose only crime seems to be that he is a mass-murderer and genocidal lunatic. It is scarcely helpful to demonise this heroic figure as a flimsy excuse for Western plans to drive the gallant people of Serbia into the sea.

Sir ALFRED SERBMAN
Independent Friends of Serbia
The Old Thatch, Belgrade

SIR—President Clinton has made a catastrophic blunder in trying to win a war by bombing alone. To be sure of victory, you have to have troops on the ground, as I discovered in Vietnam, Laos and Cambodia.

Dr HENRY KISSINGER
The Old Level Killing Field, Washington, U.S.

Why I Am So Brilliant

JOHN HUMBUG Answers Critics Of His Aggressive Interviewing Style

HOW DARE some jumped-up little journalist accuse me, the great John Humbug, of being rude to ministers about the conduct of the war?

The Today programme is a central pillar of our democratic process. Presenting it day after day is a serious undertaking, which requires courage, steadfastness and firmness of purpose.

It is vital that the British people should rally behind us at this critical time, and not sit sniping on the sidelines, writing rude articles about me.

I have made my aim in this war absolutely clear. It is to maintain a daily bombardment against the enemy, until they are forced to their knees and battered into submission by such state-of-the-art questions as "Let's face it, minister, you don't know what you're doing, do you, you twit?"

OK, so a few questions go astray and hit the wrong targets. But this is no reason why I should declare a ceasefire. I shall continue to assault these wretched politicians until they run up the white flag and say "You're right, John. I'd never have thought of that. I resign, and bless you for showing me the way."

"Why, darling, you look like a million dollars"

55

THOSE NATO KOSOVO OBJECTIVES IN FULL

1 To seek out an objective.
2 To carry out that objective successfully.
3 To remember what that objective was.
4 Er...
5 That's it.

U.S. PLEDGE TO WIN WAR 'AT ANY COST'

by Our War Correspondent **W.F. Fyffes**

THE American President, Bill Clinton, has re-affirmed his commitment to total victory in the war in Europe.

"This is a war we cannot afford to lose," he told reporters. "We will not surrender to the tinpot banana growers in the Caribbean who are attempting to defy the international convention that America can do whatever it damn well likes."

He continued, "We will not stop bombarding Europe with wave after wave of state-of-the-art American bananas — until we achieve our objective. A free market for our goods."

ALBANNANIA

The President concluded with a rousing appeal to the American people.

"I am asking you to support me against these evil islands with their sinister tropical fruits who are being aided by our enemies, such as Britain."

"We might as well finish the century as we started it"

THE EYE ASKS A GROUP OF NATIONAL FIGURES WHERE THEY STAND ON THE WAR IN KOSOVO

Julie Burchill

I am really angry and really fat. Who gives a tossover Kosover?! How dare they ask me what I think. I **don't** think. Serbs them right, anyway.

Mystic Meg

I can see the future clearly. But I can't tell you what will happen until it does.

Cilla Black

They got a lorra lorra bombs and they are going to drop them on a lorra lorra fellas! Surprise, surprise!

Billie

I mean, like, really, I mean, it's like, you know, amazing.

Archbishop Carey

You know, war is a terrible thing in a very real sense, yet in another sense all our thoughts turn to the ethnic minority Albanians. And now, Hymn No. 94.

Professor Stephen Hawking

You must buy these wonderful new spectacles, they're awfully good!

ON OTHER PAGES

Phil Space asks "Will this massive amount of coverage win the circulation war?"

PLUS: Maps, graphics, opinion, comment, but no news.

♻ NatWest   Head Office

To: Mr S. Milosevic   <u>Loan A/c No. 17234/S/DH</u>

Dear Sirb,

It has come to our attention that the above loan account, arranged in 1996, is still outstanding in the amount of £50 million.

You will recall that security for the loan comprised the following freeholds and other assets situated in the former Yugoslavia, viz:

3 bridges over Danube River
1 cement works at Milosevicograd
1 hair-dryer factory, doubling as ammunition plant
1 police headquarters
3 apartment blocks
1 NatWest bank (Tito St. branch)

We understand that these assets have recently been destroyed.

We would appreciate notification of your plans regarding repayment of the above loan at your earliest convenience.

Failure to repay this loan will inevitably result in heavy increases in charges to all our UK customers.

You have been warned.

With kind regards,

Your old friend,

Douglas

Lord Hurd of Pergua,
Manager.

SLOBODAN'S PEACE PLAN

The Albanian majority must be protected

What if we make them a minority?

Kosovo

by Our Front-Line Reporter
W.F. Deedes

Tuesday 11.10

NOT SINCE my days as a cub reporter covering the Third Crusade in 1189 have I witnessed such extraordinary scenes (contd 1194)

The Eye's Exciting New Columnist!!!

POLLY FILLER

CRISIS? What crisis? The television may be filled with desperate Kosovan refugees, but there's precious little sign of them in the Filler household.

Don't get me wrong — war is hell. Simon tells me that there hasn't been uninterrupted championship snow boarding from Kyoto on Sky 3 for nearly two whole weeks.

And if the moaning of Simon Slobbo (as I call him) wasn't bad enough, I'm having to look after Charlie the toddler because his nanny got herself fired — by me, for having her nose pierced

in Camden Market.

Honestly — doesn't the frivolous slut know there's a war on?

Anyway, so I've had to put an advert for a Kosovan girl in the Lady — having first negotiated the rudeness of their ad sales staff, one of whom brazenly asked me to spell my name out as though she'd never read a newspaper.

And guess what the response is after a whole week? Nothing. Zero. Precisely no Kosovan girls at all replying. You would have thought that every female Kosovan non-smoker with a full driving licence, no boyfriends, three years' minimum experience (NNIB preferred) and the ability to play at least one musical instrument would be beating a path to my door.

But no. Obviously, no one wants a cushy number looking after a spirited toddler (mornings and afternoons only) with the occasional five nights a week babysitting (plus weekends) and the chance to settle in with a nice family, clean their house, iron Simon's shirts and waitress at the odd dinner party.

Well, what can one say? If that is their idea of gratitude, you wonder why we have gone into this beastly war at all?
©*Polly Filler*

YES, IT'S PEACE!

by Our Political Staff
TV's Mr Lobby

THE world's longest running war came to an unexpected end yesterday when one of the combatants declared peace on the other.

In an emotional tribute to her longtime enemy Mr Heath, Lady Thatcher described him as "possibly the best prime minister this country every had between 1970 and 1974".

She singled out for special praise the election manifesto Heath offered to the nation in 1970.

"As we all know," she said, "this was an inspirational document which Mr Heath never had the courage to implement, leaving it to me to sort out, thus winning the Conservative Party three successive election victories, which is two more than he ever did, and three more than will ever be won by this pitiful little man they've got in now."

She then called on NATO to extend its bombing campaign to Mr Heath and Mr Hague, so that she could be returned to her rightful place as supreme ruler of the universe.

That Thatcher 20th Anniversary Dinner In Full

Yesterday's Men-u

Battered Squit

— ✳ —

Pickled Old Trout

— ✳ —

Sulking Pig

LABOUR TO INTRODUCE NEW-LOOK 'CRAMMER SCHOOLS'

by Our Education Staff **G.C.S.E. Failure**

MR DAVID Blunkett last night defended his new plan to introduce "crammer schools" to cater for more intelligent pupils in the state sector.

"It is quite wrong," he said, "to suggest that these are just grammar schools with one letter changed. There are in fact two letters changed."

BLUNKETT BAN

"Labour remains totally opposed to grammar schools," he went on. "In our new schools pupils will not be selected. They will be chosen, which is completely different.

"They will not be given special teaching in school, which would be divisive and iniquitous. They will be given extra teaching in schools, which is not the same thing at all.

"Our new crammer schools," he concluded, "are light years away from the discredited concept of the old grammar schools. They are as different as chalk from chalk."

THAT WOODHEAD COMPETITION

We'll wait till you leave school... how about 4pm?

THE ALTERNATIVE VOICE

Dave Spart, Assistant Deputy Chair of the National Union of Non-Teaching Delegates (Tufnell Park Branch)

... er it is utterly sickening to see the Tory Government under Mrs Margaret Blair and her henchman Blunkett attempting to impose so-called "performance related" pay on the professional teaching community, ie instituting a regime of teacher appraisal based solely on the grounds of ability viz turning the clock back to the out-moded concept of "selection", er... I mean, we as teachers do not judge our pupils on the basis of their performance in the classroom, so why should we be subjected to this... er... surely we need a fair "comprehensive" system of mixed ability teachers allowing good and bad teachers in the same schools, thus reflecting a fairer non-judgemental society... er... in fact, Mr Blunkett's performance as Education Secretary is so abysmal that he should be forced on the basis of his results to... er... hang on... er... have a pay rise... er... *(cont. p. 94)*

PRODUCT RECALL

Scottish Salmond

THE manufacturers SNP Ltd have discovered a serious defect in the above product. Anyone who is in contact with the product may well smell something rather fishy, arousing suspicions that the Salmond has "gone off" and become rotten. It must be emphasised that the Salmond is wholly unfit for general consumption and should be avoided at all costs. Do not return the Salmond to your nearest constituency, as this could lead to a mass-outbreak of Salmondella which could poison the entire United Kingdom.

TOILETS

MEN | WOMEN

MAD BOMBER SAYS 'I REGRET NOTHING'

by Our Bomb Staff
Conor Cruise O'Missile

A MAN known as "the Mad Bomber" last night confessed to launching a "campaign of terror" from his home in Downing Street, central London.

The man, known only as "Mardi Blair", admitted sending out ransom demands to a Serb businessman Mr Slobodan Massmurdovich, in which he threatened to bomb him into oblivion if he did not do what Mr Blair and his brother "Mardi Clinton" demanded.

BLAIR RAID

Eventually Blair was identified as the mastermind behind the bombings, after he was spotted every night on television.

He told the court: "These were not real threats. No one could have taken me seriously, as I had promised not to send in ground troops."

America — A Sick Society

Exclusive To All Newspapers

ONCE again, the world has been shocked by the depths of depravity to which modern America has sunk.

The United States is mired in its obsession with guns, violence and the wilder reaches of psychopathic disorder.

An ordinary suburban schoolroom is littered with the bodies of innocent schoolchildren.

Thank goodness it could not happen here, in a sleepy Scottish village, whoops, er, will this do?

On other pages: ● *Brixton Bomb — New Suspects* ● *Brick Lane — Neo-Nazis responsible?* ● *Kalashnikov shootings in Bolton* ● *Mardi Gras Bomber Sentenced* ● *Hungerford Twelve Years On* ● *Bulger Killers — New Appeal* ● *Dunblane, Could It Happen Here?* pp. 2-106

ANOTHER NATO MISTAKE

by **John Simpson**, the BBC's Global World Very-Important-Man-In-Suit Correspondent

NATO's decision to target the media is an appalling error.

Today I was taken to see the wrecked studio of Serb TV where people had been literally killed by NATO in what is meant to be a peaceful war.

But was there a more sinister motive behind this bombing? Was the real target actually me?

I was informed by one Serb insider (S. Milosevic, no relation) that NATO "will not stop until they have driven you out of Belgrade and into the rest of the country where we are busy murdering people without you noticing it".

But the whole NATO strategy of attacking myself will fail. I grow stronger in my support for myself every day. In fact, I am more committed than ever to my central aim — which is to write pieces for the Sunday Telegraph saying how important I am.

© *John Simpson*

Radio Four

The Today Programme

Sue McGhastly *(for it is she)*: The time is 7.18 and later in the programme we shall be talking to Paddy Ashdown live from Albania and Sir Leon Brittan on why 87 percent of Sweden's businessmen are saying "Yes to the Euro". And "Are warts good for you?" We'll be talking to a doctor about a new study reported in this week's Lancet. But, first, one of the most exciting archaeological discoveries in the history of the world. An old coffin has been dug up in the City of London, and it is about to be opened live, specially for this programme.

Professor Ghoul in the City, are you there? You're just about to open this coffin, and you're expecting to find something in it, aren't you?

Prof Ghoul: That's right, Sue. We're opening the coffin now.

(Creaking noise)

McGhastly: Can you see anything interesting? Dead bodies falling out of it, that kind of thing?

Ghoul: Well, only one so far. I can see some bones, dust, that sort of thing.

McGhastly: Would you say the person in the coffin had died a painful death? Could he or she have been a rape victim, possibly?

Ghoul: It's too early to say yet, Sue. There isn't really much in here. It's very old, you see.

McGhastly: But it is a genuine dead body, isn't it? Could the victim have been killed in a massacre, do you think, involving thousands of people? Or possibly murdered by a deranged psychopath while walking their dog around Roman London, and the killer never found? Well, that's all we've got time for. And now Thought For The Day, by our resident Sikh, Grobelaar Burundi.

Sikh *(for it is she)*: To those of us who watched last night's match between Manchester United and Juventus, the words of the 14th Guru *(cont'd Khz 94)*

THE INTERNUT

KenPyne

ULSTER SHOCK

We're sticking to our guns

POLICE FOLLOW UP NEW LEADS IN LAWRENCE CASE

by Our Crime Staff **Tariq Alibi**

INSPECTOR "Knacker of the Yard" Knacker last night claimed that his officers were being "deluged with phone calls" after millions of people claimed to have seen five men acting suspiciously on ITV on Thursday evening.

Said the Inspector, "We have to take these calls very seriously, as they may lead to important new clues as to the identity of Stephen's killers."

He continued, "I particularly want to talk to a coloured gentleman, a Mr Bashir, who seems to know far too much about it for his own good. I am appealing to any witnesses to come forward and identify Mr Bashir. Obviously, their names and addresses will be treated in complete confidence and published on the Internet."

GARRY BULLSHIT ON THE BOX

Did you see the lads from Eastenders on Martin Bashir's show? Didn't they do well? What a gang of loveable scamps and rogues. Come on ITV, give Jamie, Neil and Co a series.

Radio 2

What You Will Miss If They Sack Johnnie Walker

Walker *(for it is he)*: It's drive time and if you're in the Paddington area you'll be glad to know that Rita is back in business at £80 a throw and if you're on the M25 in a three mile tailback, you can get Carla to help out on 0898 76253 and... oh... and a late newsflash — the police tell me that there is a lot of congestion up my nose.

And now it's the Sniffers... sorry, the Spinners *(continued in Cell Block 94)*

"Is this your vehicle, sonny?"

POLICE

FIRST RAT EVER TO HEAD BBC

by Our Media Staff

A LONDON-BORN rodent, Mr Roland Rat, 53, is to become the first ever rat to be appointed Director-General of the BBC.

The rat has a long distinguished tail *(Surely, career in television? Ed.)*, furry whiskers and small beady eyes.

HIGH RATTINGS

Mr Rat began his broadcasting career on breakfast television, where he saved the ailing AM-TV programme with his unique blend of impromptu humour and incredibly cheap space-filling garbage.

Since then, Mr Rat's career in television has been less public, but he has held a number of distinguished positions behind the wainscoat. *(Surely, behind the scenes of some of our leading TV companies? Ed.)*

One of Mr Rat's greatest admirers is Sir Pigling Bland, the first pig ever to be chairman of the BBC.

But Sir Pigling makes it clear that the decision to appoint his friend the Rat will not be his. It will be taken by the governors who will act entirely independently in complying with his instructions to appoint the rat.

Your Drains Tonight 16

"I'd most like a One-2-One with the person I'm trying to call"

Mobile Phones Are Good For You

by Our Science Staff **James Nokia**

EARLIER fears that mobile phones can cause brain cancer and memory loss have been totally disproved by scientists.

Indeed, a new study carried out by Dr Voda Phone and Dr Cellnet of the Institute of Motorola Studies at the University of Orange proves that using a mobile phone may be actually beneficial.

The survey reveals that mobile phone use can:

● **improve mental performance by up to 1000 percent**
● **prevent hair loss**
● **increase sexual potency**
● **kill all known germs**
● **prolong life expectancy by up to 20 years.**

One To Miss

Most surprising of all was the finding that mobile phones can cause a huge increase in advertising revenue, so long as one isn't stupid enough to run silly features on the dangers of using them.

See advertisements pp. 8, 11, 12, 15, 24, 94.

IRVINE'S LEGAL REFORMS

It's my mission to take law into the 21st Century

BRITAIN'S SUPER RICH

Continued from page one)

94 Ted and Bob Spivvy
The twin brothers from Hounslow opened their first mobile phone warehouse last week and are now said to be worth £110 million. They sell on average 6,000 phones an hour and are opening new shops at a rate of 2 per minute.

95 Lord Starborgling
The 14th Earl of Corby (the "trouser press heir") inherited his father's trouser press fortune in June 1995 and has since diversified into tie and shirt presses, thus increasing the firm's annual revenue to £600 billion. He now plans to open the world's first Museum Of The Trouser Press at his ancestral home at Castle Starborgling, Yorks.

96 Tracy Poppadom
The Bradford chutney-to-samosa entrepreneur arrived in England six months ago and is already worth £200 million thanks to her revolutionary culinary concept of filling traditional samosas with Italian pizza toppings. She is the first Asian woman samosa manufacturer to make this list.

97 Nigel Nerd
The fourteen-year-old computer whizzkid from Croydon invented "Nerd 2000" in March this year, a web-search-internet-program which has made him the world's wealthiest Croydon teenager. Nerd sold his company in April to Intelquok for an estimated $200,000 million billion. He is currently working on his GCSEs.

98 HM The Queen Mother
Formerly at Number Two on the list, the Queen Mother has had a disappointing year due to injudicious investments on Lucky Lad (2.30 Uttoxeter) and Saucy Ned (3.45 Haydock Park).
(That's enough boring rich people. Ed.)

"Your hanging baskets are looking good this year, Sir Ranulf"

61

LORD ARCHER RHYMING SLANG

Romantic Fiction At Its Best

From The Pen That Brought You Heir Of Sorrows And Love In The Saddle

BORN TO BE QUEENY

by Sylvie Krin

The love story of the decade that dare not speak its name!

THE STORY SO FAR: The dashing young Tony Blair, leader of the New Labour Party, has won the heart of the whole nation — and not just the nation! Behind the scenes, his two closest friends are vying desperately for his affection. It was a ménage à trois from hell...

Now read on...

"Don't you ever speak to me like that again, Gordy." The front door of Number Ten slammed shut with a sickening crash, as the svelte Minister Without Portfolio flounced out into the night.

The burly constable on the door sighed.

"Good night, Mr Mandelson," he cried cheerily.

"No, it jolly well isn't. It's perfectly horrid. That's the last time I'll ever help Tony again."

And with that he was gone, leaving only a faint fragrance of Giverny Pour L'Homme on the evening air.

Back in the elegant drawing room, the handsome young Prime Minister sobbed quietly, with his head in his hands.

"Don't take on so, Tony," soothed the saturnine young Scotsman, whose mastery of finance had won the admiration of the entire world, placing a comforting hand on his leader's shoulder.

"I just can't understand it, Gordy," gulped the Prime Minister. "Why can't you and Mandy get on? You've got so much in common — me, for instance."

"That's just it," protested the beetle-browed son of the manse. "It's come to the point where you've got to choose between us. We can't go on like this."

"Don't make me choose, Gordon," responded the tousle-haired inventor of the Third Way. "It's just not fair to any of us. You know I love you both equally. Let's not throw it all away, all that we've dreamed of and hoped for and planned for and longed for..."

His voice trailed off disconsolately.

"You're right, Prime Minister. My feelings got the better of me. Beneath this dour and prudent exterior beats the heart of a passionate man. Och, aye, the Noo Labour." He broke into his distinctive Lowland brogue.

At that very moment the door burst open, and there stood a motor-cycle messenger, clad entirely in black leather, holding a letter marked "Extremely Personal". "I'm a friend of Peter's," he said. "Which one of you is the Prime Minister?"

With one voice, Tony and Gordie chorused, "I am."

"Oh, sorry, I was forgetting myself," Gordon went on embarrassingly.

But Tony had already snatched at the pink missive, eagerly tearing it open and running his eyes avidly down its contents.

"My dearest Prime Minister," he read to himself. *"I cannot tell you how upset I was tonight over our silly disagreement on whether we should charge VAT on child benefit. I can't believe that you sided with Gordon, after all we have meant to each other. Honestly, to suggest a rate of five-and-a-half percent is nothing more than a slap in the face, making a complete mockery of our friendship. I don't mind telling you, Tony, that Gordon has to go — or I will. There, I've said it! It's up to you now, dearest heart. Be strong. Be kind. Be sensible. Vote Labour. You know it makes sense. Your loving friend, Mandy."*

"Well, what does he say?" asked the gruff denizen of Number 11. "Is he apologising for his unforgivable rudeness in daring to challenge my plans to harmonise VAT across a whole range of benefits?"

"Yes, it's a wonderful letter," replied the blue-eyed statesman, hurriedly scrunching up the note and cramming it into his pocket.

"He wants us all to work together as we used to in the old days. It's going to be such fun, isn't it, Gordon?"

"Aye, I'll drink to that," responded the cautious Scotsman, a sardonic little smile round his finely chiselled mouth. "You can rely on me, Tony."

"You can rely on me, Tony. That was a wonderful letter you wrote me. I don't mind telling you, I've got tears in my eyes."

Mandy eased back into the specially-made Habitat white leather sofa, in the drawing room of his luxurious Notting Hill maisonette. He gazed down at the precious note, written out in the Prime Minister's own hand, and read it for the fourth time.

"Dearest Minister, Please, please don't be cross with me. Gordon has apologised for all the beastly things he said to you about VAT. You know, he didn't mean it. We mustn't behave like people in one of those horrid Greek tragedies, like the one where Achilles sulks in his tent and lets the Trojans win. No, we're all going to work together from now on. Let tomorrow be the start of the rest of our lives. We shall be the Three Musketeers. Remember? One for all, and all for me. Gordos, Mandos and Blairtagnan!! It's going to be such fun. All my loving, Your friend and Prime Minister, Tony."

Mandy's tears of joy dropped softly onto the Number Ten headed paper. He had misjudged Gordon. It was all going to be alright.

"It's all going to be alright! I've got the document right here." Gordy was talking quietly into his mobile phone.

At the other end of the line, an excited journalist could scarcely contain himself. "We'll have to hold the front page for this one," he enthused. "It'll be the scoop of the year."

"Of course, I'm sorry for Mandy," rasped the menacing tones of the latter day Bismarck of finance. "But it was an unforgiveable error of judgement on his part, for which he deserves to pay the full price."

"You mean, accepting the £373,000 loan from Geoffrey Robinson for his luxury Notting Hill penthouse?" queried the eager hack.

"Och, no," replied Gordie, his face lighting up for the first time in months with a wintry smile. "Trying to come between me and Tony..."

© *Sylvie Krin, The Trouser Press, Old Compton Street, Soho*

HRH The Queen & Prince Philip
Invite You All To

Foot The Bill For

The Marriage Between
HRH Prince Edward
And
Miss Sophie Rhys-Jones
On 19th June

OLD LADY SCALDS FOOT IN BATH

by Our Global Tragedy Staff **John Simpson**

Mustique, Wednesday

A 68- YEAR-OLD divorcee has suffered a burnt foot after getting into a hot bath without checking the temperature of the water first. Paramedics rushed to the scene and her condition is now described as satisfactory *(P.A.)*

A Nation's Shame

by **Linda Lee-Potty**

How could we let an old-age pensioner living alone on her paradise island get into a bath with no supervision from the Social Services? What kind of country have we become?

As the islanders tried to come to terms with their tragedy, one said, "It was an accident waiting to happen."

Meanwhile, in London, a demonstration outside Number Ten Downing Street demanded an immediate ban on "Killer Hot Baths" for Britain's elderly. And about time too.

How many more old ladies will it take before Blair acts?

Ring our Hot Bath Line now on 78-79-80-81-Phew, what a scalder!

Deadly bath of the type believed to have been involved in the old lady's brush with death.

RIP
OLIVER REED
SADLY
PISSED

"Father, I've got an Asda loyalty card and I shopped at Tesco"

NEW-LOOK QUEEN
(part 94)

Get me trainers, Phil — me feet are killin' me!

COURT CIRCULAR

BUCKINGHAM PALACE
His Royal Highness the Prince William will attend a discotheque-dance to celebrate the eighteenth birthday of the Honourable Sophie Caroline O'Kay-Yargh, the niece once-removed of the Mistress Royal, Camilla Parker Knowles.

The Prince will be accompanied by a number of old Etonians and will consume cocktails known as "Hogwhimperers" in the Sloane Bar before asking Lady Tarara-Boomdeay for a snog by the payphones.

Carriages will be at 3.30am and the procession will be composed as follows:

First Taxi
HRH Prince William
Second Taxi
Charlie Twoshort-Planques and Rupert St John "Bollox" Harcourt
Third Taxi
Misses Binty, Bunty, Minty, Mandy and Minky de la Vere Oranjeeboom
First Bottom Out Of The Window
The Rt Hon Henry Hooray-Lycett-Moon
Second Bottom Out Of The Window
Johnny de la Vere "Pubes" Featherstone-Haugh
First Photographer On Moped
Richard Beardie of the Picture Agency BUM
(That's enough. Ed.)

COMING OUT SOON

NOTTING HILL

The romantic comedy sensation of the summer — a young floppy-haired English spin doctor called Peter falls in love with the incredibly famous American-style Prime Minister, Tony. Their will they/won't they relationship charmingly explores the ups and downs of a love affair between an obscure lad from Hartlepool and an international megastar. Will they live happily ever after or will Peter get sacked as soon as he is no longer useful? Watch out for a wonderful cameo by Peter's stuccoed house in Notting Hill which is central to the film's plot.

Cast In Full

Peter . . . . .HUGH GRANT
Tony . . . . .JULIA ROBERTS

From the team that brought you **Four Sackings and a Resignation!**

METROPOLITAN POLICE

Murder Hunt — 26th April

If you have any information about, or witnessed any news coverage of, the cold-blooded murder of hundreds of people in the Balkans, or other similar human tragedies which did not occur in West London on the above date — then you were probably not watching or listening to BBC News.

THE TIMES FRIDAY MAY 14 1999

What Jill's Killer Would Have Seen

BY TIMES CORRESPONDENT PHIL SPACE

THE number 94 bus, identified yesterday by Inspector Knacker at an identity parade of buses as the getaway bus used by the killer of TV presenter Jill Dando, operates one of London's most popular bus routes, passing such famous landmarks as the Neasden bus garage, the fountains in Trafalgar Square, Wembley Stadium and the Muswell Hill Tesco.

Had Jill's killer sat upstairs, as seems increasingly likely, he could well have enjoyed a "top deck" view of many of London's most popular tourist sites.

What he would have seen:

☐ Buckingham Palace, home of Britain's Queen;

☐ 37 Graythorpe Gardens, birthplace of carrot-haired TV mogul Chris Evans;

☐ The Duke of Ellington, fashionable jazz pub in Elephant and Castle (formerly The Slug and Lettuce);

☐ Chelsea's Toast Shop, the world's only emporium dedicated to the art of toastmaking;

☐ Notting Hill Underground Station, as seen in the hit film *Four Weddings And A Tube Station.*

This is a journey the TV presenter's killer would never have forgotten — and nor must we.

Wish You Were Still Here?

By PHILIPPA PAGE

WHAT made her so extraordinary was precisely that she was so ordinary.

It was her very ordinariness that made her so extraordinary.

In an age when *(cont'd in all newspapers)*

975 AD

ST CHARLES OF MOORE becomes editor of the *Anglo-Saxon Chronicle,* taking over from former editor The Venerable Deedes.

He revolutionises the design, removing accounts of old style ecclesiastic events and replacing them with new style reports of rape and pillage in Wessex *(see Page III)*.

Also introduces front cover illuminations of semi-clad wenches, notably Elizabeth of Hurley. Perhaps best known for weekly sermons on the important issues of the day, such as "Are hair shirts being worn long this year?", "How celibacy can improve your love life" and "Are madrigals the new rock and roll?" *(Surely 'Gregorian Plainsong'? Ed.)*

Fell from grace due to his resisting closer ties with Europe (ie Norman invasion) and was declared a martyr by loyal followers in Tunbridgium (now Tunbridge Wells).

© AD (Anno Dominic)

"My biggest fear is all our copiers going haywire on Millennium Eve"

I've got post-NATO depression

NATO PRACTISE RANGE

Conflict In The Balkans
Briefing
Day 94

■ NATO attacks military installation in Belgrade. Ice cream van in Pristina is successfully destroyed.

■ Clinton regrets civilian casualties, but promises "The war will go on until it stops."

■ Pentagon sends warship, USS Enterprise, to Balkans. "Its five year mission," according to Admiral James T. Kirk, "to boldly go where no man has gone before (except not into Kosovo, obviously)".

■ Pentagon admits USS Enterprise has sunk on training exercise after collision with Klingon Vessel.

■ NATO send in F-94 super stealth laser-guided Smart Bombers to attack targets in Skopje.

■ 5,000 refugees flee to Macedonia to escape accidental death at hands of F-94 super stealth laser-guided Smart Bombers.

■ NATO unveils new strategy to attack civilian targets in hope of hitting some Serb soldiers.

A Cab Driver Writes
for the Sunday Telegraph

Every week a taxi driver is invited to comment on an issue of topical importance.

This week: The War In Serbia by Andy Roberts (Cab No. 666).

BLIMEY! See what those Serbs have done now, guv? They're making bloody fools of us. I mean that NATO is bloody useless innit? Blair, Clinton, bunch of tossers, if you ask me! Worse than bloody Chamberlain signing up to Munich in September 1938, know what I mean?

Anyway, know what I'd do with that Slobodan Milosawotsit? Drop the atom bomb on Belgrade. Nuke the Serbs, that's what I say! It's the only language they understand. It certainly brought the Nips to heel and made Admiral Yamomoto get on board the USS Missouri double quick to kiss McArthur's arse, pardon my Serbo-Croat. No, guv'nor, stop mucking about, let's go nuclear.

Do you want a receipt, guv? I 'ad that Winston Churchill in the back of my book once. Now there was a real prime minister...

© The Sunday Telegraph

Dave Spart, Co-Chair SNNN (Stop The NATO Nazis Now), Tufnell Park Branch

The Imperialist warmongers, ie, Adolf Clinton and Tony Himmler, have finally emerged in their true colours in their deliberate murder of innocent Chinese diplomats from a country with which we have no quarrel whatsoever, er... we would like to express solidarity with our student comrades in condemning this disgraceful and wanton violence against a nation that is internationally known for its stand on Human Rights and its genocide in Tibet... er... er... er... (Cont'd p. 94)

THE VICE PRESIDENT SPEAKS OUT

How dare they kill innocent Chinese people? That's our job

胡锦涛发表重要电视讲话

"That's the trouble with targets – they all look the same to me"

CHINESE EMBASSY HIT

WE REVEAL THE 'SCOOP' ADDICTS – Slaves To A Craving They Cannot Control

By The Eye's Investigative Reporter N. TRAPMENT

THEY LIVE in a twilight world of criminality, vice and big money. They are the "scoop" addicts who need a weekly "fix" merely to survive.

In a squalid warehouse in Wapping we spoke to one pathetic employee of the News of the World, who had travelled all the way to the South of France to "score".

COKE CANNES

She told us, "I had to pretend to be a fresh young party-goer in order to get the dope on Tom Parker-Bowles.

"I hadn't had a story in weeks, and I was desperate. I would have done anything.

"Luckily, I met this bloke who knew this bloke who rang some other bloke on his mobile, who fixed me up with just what I needed.

"All I had to do was go up to this young hooray, and say 'I really fancy you. Can you get me some coke, and I'll show you a nice time.'

"He said, 'er, yes, OK, I think I might know some chap I was at Eton with, who does that sort of thing.'

"Immediately I felt a rush of euphoria which is difficult to describe in words. I was on a real high. It is something you only get with really high-grade stuff."

SNOW BUSINESS

This poor girl is only one of a small army of misfits, drop-outs and social rejects who hang around Wapping, with their shadowy "Mr Big", or "Mr Dig", as he is known.

Another addict we spoke to described the almost incredible lengths to which he had gone to inject some life into his pathetic newspaper.

"I dressed up as an Arab," he confessed, "and spent weeks following this BBC DJ around in the hope that he would give me what I wanted.

"Finally, he delivered, and it was real top-grade shit, even if it did cost hundreds of thousands of pounds of Rupert Murdoch's money."

WOODY ADOPTS DAUGHTER

Just think, in ten years' time I can marry her

"Possession of an offensive weapon and suspected drug dealing – six months!"

School News

St Cokes

Eton Term begins today. There are 278 boys in jail. JRD Nose-Candy (Snorters) is Head of Sniffers. RLP Snow-Job (Dealers) is Keeper Of The Silver Spoon. There will be an inspection of the school by Superintendent PRV Truncheon (O.C.) who will arrest most of the Upper Sixth. Drugs will be run on June 4th through Founder's Nose. The Parker Bowl, awarded for Inter-House Peddling, has been won by PLJ Substance-Abuse (Charlies). Overdoses are on 31st June.

COURT CIRCULAR

HIGHGROVE
HRH The Prince of Wales will give a lecture on "The Dangers Of Drug Abuse" to an invited audience of his two sons, HRH Prince William and HRH Prince Harry. The Princes will shuffle nervously, look at the floor and display signs of embarrassment as their father discusses matters about which they know more than he does.

HRH The Prince Of Wales will then deliver a second lecture by telephone to the son of the Mistress Royal, Mr Thomas Coker-Knows, on "The Dangers Of Speaking To The Popular Press". The Royal Equerry, Air Vice-Commodore Archibald Trumper-Smythe will then replace the receiver on the cradle, before ringing the Press Association to acquaint them with the details of the above exchanges.

BUCKINGHAM PALACE
HRH the Duke of Edinburgh will grant an audience to Mr Gyles Brandreth, the former television personality and Conservative MP, in which he will attempt to answer a barrage of fearless and probing questions such as "Would it be right to say, Your Majesty, that no one has done more than you, sire, to uphold the institution of monarchy?"

THEN AND NOW — HUNTER

This next play has got some kissing in it – you'd better send the children to bed...

This next play features incest, sodomy and rape – you'd better send Granny to bed!

CELEBRITY DID NOT TAKE COCAINE

An Eye Exclusive

The Return of Christopher Columbus

by Our Investigative Reporters **Sheik Itall-Abott** (Reg Filth) and the **Rt Hon Arabella Foxtrot** (Tracy Slapper) with additional reporting by **Sharon Tart**

A WELL-KNOWN celebrity has admitted to Private Eye that he has never taken cocaine nor sold any to his friends.

This extraordinary revelation could well end his career and has sent out shockwaves through the world of showbusiness.

In a classic honey-bee sting, our reporters taped a late night conversation with the famous star of stage, screen and sports field.

Here is the incredible transcript of shame:

Slapper: One two testing testing… Oh hello! Fancy a legover, big boy – I'm all yours.

Just get me some stuff, ie cocaine, an A grade drug with a street value of £4 million.

Celeb: I beg your pardon. Have we been introduced?

Slapper: Come up to my bedroom for a steamy love romp just so long as you get the stuff, okay?

Celeb: Goodness me, look at the time. I must get home, I'm doing the school run tomorrow. Well, good evening, a pleasure to meet you…

But the star's agent angrily denied that his client was "squeaky clean" or free from "the taint of sleaze".

"It was a one-off," protested the agent. "He was tired, he had been working hard. It was a lapse, for God's sake."

But last night the celebrity refused to comment further and (continued page 2, 3, 4, 5, 6, 7, 8 and 94)

POLLY FILLER

"MY NOTTING HILL"

WHEN I first moved to London I could easily have ended up in Notting Hill. This was in pre-Slobbo days (ie, when I wasn't living with the useless Simon) and when Charlie wasn't even a drunken twinkle in Simon's eyes after he had spent the night watching Juventus vs. Quattroformaggio at the Bar Italia.

No, I was young, free, single and very attractive and Notting Hill was where people like me wanted to be.

With its leafy garden centres, quaint, Victorian shopping malls and the celebrated antique fish market in Camden Passage Road, Notting Hill is the quintessential London village. Where else can you find blue doors on Regency mews terraces and cobbled stucco façades under Georgian railway arches? Where else are you likely to bump into Peter Mandelson, Richard Curtis and Madonna, all buying Algerian coffee at the Cafe Guevarra on the corner of Portobello Avenue and Westbourne Square?

No, Notting Hill has always been unique. But is it still unique now that "That Film" has put it so firmly on the map?

I WENT back and wandered around what would have been my old haunts (if I hadn't decided to buy a flat in Battersea instead and then move to Streatham in the hope of getting more of a garden).

So, I followed in the footsteps of Hugh Grant and Julia Roberts, browsing through the shelves of the second-hand flower stalls and finally, like them, buying a croissant from the old Greek bakery next to the Baptist Tabernacle Mission Centre across the road from Asda.

So, has it changed? I would have to say "Yes, it has" in some ways, but in other ways it remains the same Notting Hill I never knew.

©*Polly Filler*

THAT HUGH GRANT INTERVIEW

A Private Eye Digest Service Reprinted from all newspapers.

Floppy hair… charming… engaging smile… gosh… floppy hair… boyish good looks… public school accent… floppy hair… Liz Hurley's dress… unfortunate incident in Los Angeles… er… gosh… floppy hair… ghastly journalists aways writing about how marvellous I am… er… that's it.

© *Notting Hype*

THE NEW POLITICS
WHY BRITAIN WILL NEVER LOOK THE SAME AGAIN

by Political Staff **Phil Space**

"It's the first time in 300 years we've been able to register our apathy"

THEY said it would never happen. But on May 6th 1999 it did. The political landscape was inexorably changed once and for all. In a historic 24 hours that shook the world the face of British Politics was irrevocably redrawn in an extraordinary revolution that swept aside centuries of tradition.

Not since the Battle of Bannockburn when Mel McGibson surrendered to the overwhelming might of King Edward the Fox has this sceptred isle seen anything to match this momentous day. *(Keep going. Ed. Only seven pages left to fill.)*

As dawn broke over the battlements of Edinburgh Castle, a lone figure stood silhouetted against the blood-red sky.

For, on this man's shoulders the mantle of Scottish greatness will sit, the latest in a long line of larger-than-life Scottish heroes. Their ghosts seemed to parade before him — Robert the Bruce, Macbeth, Sir Walter Scott, Kenneth McKeller, Logie Baird, Andy Stewart and his Band, William McGonnagal, Stanley Baxter, Ian McKaskill.

And now, there he was, the heir to greatness: Donald Dewar *(Who he? Ed.)*

HOW THE NEW POLITICS WORKS

The sterile old-style politics of opposition has gone for ever. In one fell swoop Tony Blair has created a new way of governing Britain. He promised reform and now we have it.

Out Goes
● **Yah-boo style confrontation.**

In Comes
● **Meaningful dialogue resulting in consensus.**

Out Goes
● **Old-style first-past-the-post majority government.**

In Comes
● **New-style proportional representation allowing all parties a fair say in the way Britain is run.**

The first example of the new politics in action occurred in the Sean Connery Suite of the Caledonian Travel Lodge at a historic meeting of the Scottish Labour and Liberal Democrats who met over McDonald's McMuffins and carbonated Highland Spring water to decide Scotland's future in a civilised, modern way that is a million miles from the backbiting world of Westminster politicking. Said the newly elected Donald Dewar: "There will be no deal with the sandal-wearing beardies unless they shut up and do what I tell them."

The LibDemocrat leader Hugh McHee agreed, saying "There will be no deal with Tony's toadies unless they drop tuition fees, give us the best jobs and do what we tell them."

The meeting later broke up after a short fight which was continued in a nearby pub.

Those Scottish Election Results In Full

Auchtermuchty South
(Turnout 6)

Angus McLoonie (Kill All Sassenachs Party) 2; Arran McSweater (Liberal McDemocrat Alliance) 2; Jimmy McTimeserver (Old Labour) 1; Heather McBroccoli (Scottish Greens) 1; Harry Twistleton-Phipps-Farquhar (Conservative and Unionist) 0. No change. *(That's enough results. Ed.)*

Those Welsh Election Results In Full

Pontymeithon
(Turnout 1)

Llewellyn Lloonie (Burn English Cottages Party) 0; Daffyd Duck (Lllliberal Democratic Party); Ron Davies (Brixton Dinner Party) 0; Tarquin Twistleton-Phipps-Farquhar (Conservative and Unionist) 0; Simon Heffer (English Independence From Wales) 0; Screaming Lord Sheep 1; Ron Davies swings both way. *(That's enough Welsh Elections. Ed.)*

Those English Election Results In Full

(Cont'd p. 94)

HISTORY MADE AS DEWAR UNVEILS TEAM

by Our Scottish Political Staff **Lunchtam O'Shanter**

Edinburgh, Tuesday

HISTORY was made again today when, after two weeks of tough, behind-the-scenes bargaining, Donald Dewar, Scotland's first ever First Minister, announced to an astonished world what he called "the most impressive Scottish political team ever assembled in Scotland".

That top Dewar team in full:

● **Donny Dewar**, 75, King of Scotland, Lord of the Isles and former husband of the wife of the Laird of Lairg (Derry Irvine).

● **Jim McLoon**, 41, Lib Dem Deputy First-King and Thane of Cawdor, with special responsibility for safety in the workplace.

● Ms **Sheena McShona**, 32, high-flying former dental hygienist who now steps up to take on the tricky, Heath, Sport, Croft Develop-ment and Racial Awareness in the Fisheries Industry portfolio.

● **Patsy McSweater**, 33, a friend of Gordon Brown's secretary's aunt, who formerly worked in the Dumfries Libraries Department, now takes on the pivotal post of Minister for Coordinating Internet Development, Tourism and Puffin Control.

● **Menzies McThingus**, 46, Lib Dem elder statesman, who graduates from his former post as Co-Chair of the Lothian Business Link Development Partnership to become Minister for Highland Games, Drug Enforcement and Solar Windfarms.

Said Dewar, as he introduced his team to the world's waiting newsmen, "Make no mistake. These are the men, women and Liberal Democrats who are going to forge Scotland into a country fit for the 21st century.

"Full details," he said, "can be found on the Home Rule page of our new website www.scotbore.co.notuk"

SCOTLAND'S DAY OF DESTINY

So how many people turned out to vote?

007

Cricket World Cup
Six To Watch

THE Eye's cut-out-and-keep guide to the top stars who will set the world of one-day cricket asleep *(Surely "alight"? Ed.)*.

Veridojeebowlah
Sri Lanka's wily spinmeister whose lethal armoury includes the off-break, the googly, the throw, the chuck and the obvious no ball.

Eye Rating: 9 for 33

Wazi Akruk
Pakistan's "Mr Nice" currently facing 11 charges of match fixing and bribery. A good bet if you've paid him.

Eye Rating: 3 years' suspended sentence

Weit Van de Druyver
South Africa's fiery paceman. Can always be identified by his white sun-block, "Don't want to look like a Keffir" he quips.

Eye Rating: PG

Patak Tandoorinan
India's master batsman — he can cope with anything that is thrown at him — including coins, bottles and fire bombs.

Eye Rating: Very Hot

Bruce Blimey
Australia's hardhitting Number 4 batsman who is always willing to thump the opposition around the ground — although he is not so good with the bat.

Eye Rating: 58 (People Retired Hurt)

Moses Wellington
The West Indie's demon bowler is 7ft 7in tall and delivers the ball at an astonishing 173 miles an hour — pretty fast for a leg spinner. Soon to join the NATO squad for the aerial bombardment of Belgrade.

Eye Rating: Ow!

Andy Useless
England's all-rounder, equally hopeless at batting, bowling and fielding. Needs to lose some weight if he isn't to make a huge impression on the pitch.

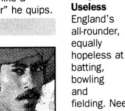

Eye Rating: 19 stone

(That's enough cricketers. Ed.)

NEW-LOOK QUEEN Pt 94

I'll have a chicken korma, two naan and a pint of lager

AND IF YOU DON'T WANT TO SEE THE ENGLAND INNINGS — LOOK AWAY NOW

GLENDA SLAGG

Fleet Street's Honey-Crap *(Surely 'trap'? Ed.)*

HANDS OFF Lenny Henry, all you sleazy-so-called-journalists!?!?! What's he ever done to deserve this??!?

OK, so he had a blonde bimbo in his hotel room and he had a bit of a laugh with some good-time gals at a Lap Dance Club!?!? SO WHAT???!

Lenny's a lively lad who likes to live life to the full!??! What kind of hypocrites have we all become when we ruin his marriage just to make a headline and sell a newspaper?? The price on the front page should be thirty pieces of silver!?! Perhaps the Editor should take a leaf out of the Bible and hang himself!?!? Geddit??! *(It was me. You're fired. Ed.)*

LENNY HENRY – what a skunk!! No wonder poor Dawn is a-weepin' and a-wailin' at his love-rat shenanigans!?! Who do you think you are??! Just 'cos you work for charity doesn't mean you can cheat on your lovely wife, the Vicar of Dibley?!?!

So much for your model showbiz marriage!??! What kind of hypocrite are you Lenny, or should I say *Judas*??? You should go away with your 30 pieces of crumpet and hang yourself!??! *(Much better, but it needs to be even more unpleasant before you're hired again. Ed.)*

DAWN FRENCH – no wonder your hubby's playing away from home when you are so fat!!! A gal who lets her figure go, has only herself to blame when a responsible newspaper exposes her hubby as a two-timing bonkaholic!?!??

Take some well-meant advice from Auntie Glenda, Dawn dearie

– lose twenty stone or lose your fella instead?!? *(Alright, you're hired again. Ed.)*

THREE CHEERS for Dawn French?!?! She's not going to slim down just because the media tell her to!! We love you just the way you are, Dawn – Jumbo sized and Roly-Poly!!! Go on, Dawn, keep eating and prove the world wrong!??! *(You're fired again. Ed.)*

HERE THEY are, Glenda's Mid-summer Madmen!!?!

Paul Scholes – First England player to be sent off at Wembley! Come and play dirty round at my place, ducks! (Geddit?)

Huw Edwards – The BBC's Mr Sex O'Clock News!! Ok, you may be a turn off to the viewers, Taffy, but I think you're to Dai. for!?!? Geddit??!?

Martti Ahtissaari – Crazy name, crazy guy!!
That's the Finnish – Geddit??!?!

Byeeeee!

71

Apology
THE SERBS

IN recent weeks, in common with all other newspapers, we may have given the impression that the Serbs were a ferocious fighting people, whose long history of gallant resistance to outside invasion had shown them to be astonishingly brave in the face of adversity. Such men, it may have been inferred, would only have had their resolve hardened to fine-tempered steel by the counter-productive aerial bombardments by NATO. Headlines such as "Plucky Serbs Dig In For Long Haul", "Hitler's 250 Divisions Could Not Tame Johnny Serb" and "Serbs Rally Behind Super-Slobbo" may have led readers to believe that the Serbs were in some fashion invincible and would fight to the death in support of their leader.

We now realise that there was not a jot or scintilla of truth in these allegations, and that the Serbs are merely a bunch of drunken gangsters who will turn tail at the thought of anything more taxing than murdering unarmed civilians, before removing their videos and fridges to Belgrade. We further realise that any close study of the history of the Balkans would immediately reveal that the Serbs' capacity to lose every war they have ever fought is equalled only by that of NATO. We would like to apologise for any confusion caused by our earlier reports.

PCC Ruling

BLONDE SEX BOMB TRAPS MARRIED MEDIA MAN!

MEDIA LOVE RAT DUMPS MISSUS FOR SEXY STUNNER!

BIG PIX OF MEDIA HEIR'S BRIDE'S TITS INSIDE!

The Major/Noble Wedding Breakfast Of The Century

(as exclusively reported in the Daily Hellograph)

That Slapper-Up Meal In Full

Dim Son

— ✳ —

Fruity Tart With No Dressing
(That's enough. Ed)

War Briefing
Week 94

☐ Monday. NATO bombs Swedish Embassy, two hospitals and teddy bear factory in Novi Sad.

☐ Tuesday. NATO spokesman Jamie Shea apologies for bombing Swedish Embassy and hospitals, but defends attack on teddy bear factory on grounds that a 1954 Blue Guide to Novi Sad had shown it as a "key military installation".

☐ Wednesday. Blair flies out to Macedonia to promise "every Kosovar refugee child will be given a teddy bear by NATO". Three more US Apache helicopters crash on training mission to drop teddy bears onto camps.

☐ Thursday. NATO bombs Romania, mistaking it for Bulgaria. Robin Cook and Madeline Albright appear on thousands of television programmes. Says Cook, "Milosevic is cracking up. He keeps going on TV to claim he is winning."

☐ Friday. Luxembourg foreign minister calls for an end to ground war and pledges that not a single Luxembourg soldier will be sent into Kosovo.

☐ Saturday. John Simpson predicts sunny spell with occasional rain, based on information from "Belgrade government sources" (S. Milosevic). It snows all day.

☐ Sunday. NATO warplanes attack Belgrano, killing hundreds of innocent Argentine fish. Jamie Shea explains the bombs had been targeted on Belgrade, which was "only three letters out — not a bad ratio, considering the number of cock-ups we have made". *(To be continued)*

SOLDIER ANTS

MEDIA ANTS

WORLD EXCLUSIVE

THOSE MI6 NAMES IN FULL

as anonymously revealed on the Internet by top-secret website www.fugginlies.harrods.co.uk

1 **Her Majesty the Queen** (code name "Brenda"). Known to have personally ordered the murder of Princess Diana and Prince Dodi.

2 **HRH the Duke of Edniburgh** (code name "Keith"). Colluded in the brutal murder of Diana and Dodi.

3 **His Royal Highness the Prince of Wales** (code name "Brian"). Known to have personally been the driver of the white Fiat Uno which caused the fatal crash leading to the above murders.

4 **Tom Bower** (code name "Fuggin' Bastard"). Hired by the Queen to assassinate the character of His Royal Highness Mohamed Al-Fayed of That Shop.

5 **Jack Straw** (code name "Labour Pooftah"). Conspired with fellow poofs to deny British passport to HRH Mohamed Al-Fayed.

6 **Lord So-Called Norman Tebbit** (code name "Ungrateful Shit"). Took gifts from generous Middle Eastern benefactor and then bad-mouthed him in the press.

7 **R.W. Rowland** (code name "Tiny"). Faked own death in order to work undercover for HM The Queen in her plans to prevent the rightful award of a passport to His Supreme Holiness the Dalai Fayed.

8 **Dominic Lawson** (code name "Rosa's Husband"). Expert in black propaganda who uses his newspaper to discredit *(cont'd. website 94)*

MEN'S SUMMERWEAR FROM RACING GNOME

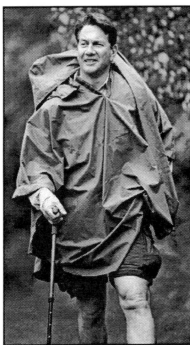

Photograph of model taken on the pilgrim route to Santa Miguela di Fotopportuniti

The Portillo

Stylish, Spanish-look rainproof kagool, ideal for the man who is going places (£2.99). Plus matching, elastic-wasted, above-the-knee shorts, in figure-hugging Torytex (£6.99). Plus solid, hardwood, all-purpose stick with which to beat William Hague (£32.99).

"For The Man Who Isn't Wet"

TV Highlights

ITV 10.00 pm
Tonight With Trevor Barbados
The hard-hitting current affairs show continues to lift the lid on contemporary issues. Tonight it's:
● *Exploding Toasters — Have the IRA discovered a new secret weapon?*
● *Fake Opticians — Are your glasses really made out of GM plastic?*
● *The Sex Trade — How the TV men exploit the pornographers for their own purposes.*

BBC1 7.30 pm
Trolley Rage
Secret supermarket CCTV footage of dangerous outbursts of trolley rage in the nation's shopping aisles. Watch Britain's shoppers run amok. Includes stabbing, murder, and multiple trolley pile-ups resulting in thousands of deaths.

9.00pm BBC1
The Lift Men From Hell
Britain's most offensive lift operators are revealed in a frightening new fly-on-the-ceiling docu-soap from the makers of Petrol Pump Attendants From Hell. This week Eric, senior lift operator in Bentalls, Neasden, traps an elderly gentleman's scarf in the door.

8.00pm Carlton
Paranormal Pets
Can spiders predict the future? Roger's pet tarantula, Mystic Monty, accurately foresaw the bombing of the Chinese Embassy by NATO and has also won the lottery ten times. *(That's enough TV. Ed.)*

Which of us is in charge of Scotland?

I'll have to ask Mr Blair

"And when they touch you, you get this wonderful feeling of stupidity and ignorance"

NURSERY TIMES

FRIDAY JUNE 25 1999

"I DON'T WANT A FAIRYTALE WEDDING," says Snow White

by Our Royal Correspondent
Humpty Dumpster

SNOW WHITE has defied tradition and opted for a low-key wedding to Prince Charming. Ms White has decided to keep her own name rather than become Princess Charming and will carry on with her successful career as a dwarf consultant.

"I will obviously support my husband in his work as the managing director of Charming Productions, but I see no reason why this marriage should stop me both whistling and working in the dwarf field."

Ms White continued: "I will not be another Cinderella. No one can replace Cinders as a national icon and I am not going to try."

Ms White then told waiting reporters from the Nursery Times pool, "We are hoping to avoid the pitfalls of previous fairytale weddings and to live happily ever after."

ON OTHER PAGES

- Raunchy Pictures Of Snow White's Apples p. 2
- My Night In The Forest With Snow White by The Huntsman p. 3
- The Dangers Of Genetically Modified Beanstalks by Prince Charmless p. 94

Happy, Darling?

Yes – Fergie's not here

Old Snob Writes

THE TITLE of the Earl of Wessex dates back to 738 AD when the Kingdom of Wessex was ruled over by King Egcup. When the Kingdom merged with the Fiefdom of Fergia in 872 the title became that of hereditary Thane held in the gift of the new Monarch of Middle England King Nobert the Daft (related to Prince Edward through his niece Queen Grunhilde von Liebfraumilch).

The title fell into desuetude for several centuries, but was revived by Prince Albert when it was bestowed on his 18th son, the Duke Duke of Earl, on the occasion of his marriage to Princess Petra von Schmeichel in 1837.

The Queen's imaginative gesture in reviving this ancient title is to be commended, signalling as it does the Queen's ambition to take the Monarchy forward into the eleventh century.

© Old Snob, The Telegraph Group

THAT DRESS IN FULL

by Our Fashion Correspondent
Princess Alexandra of Shulman

IT WAS the dress that stole the show. A daring symphony of texture and colour which upstaged every other frock in the chapel.

Make no mistake about it, the assembled guests only had eyes for the Bishop of Norwich. This flaming red silk and satin chasuble with matching heavily embroidered stole had fashion correspondents gasping.

Praise My Stole The King Of Heaven

It was designed by Mrs Fiona Dunwoody, 68, and her team of lady helpers from the Norwich WI.

"I saw the material in John Lewis and I thought to myself that it would be perfect for the Bishop on her big " she said.

The high street shops are already experiencing huge demands for copy-cat vestments and there can be no doubt what the best-dressed vicars will be wearing this summer.

Said a spokesman for High Street fashion giants *World of Chasubles*, "We have been inundated by a phone call from Rev Peabody in Nuneaton already." *(Cont. p. 94)*

How To Remember Those Royal Brides

by Henry VIII

Divorced
Divorced
Divorced

Divorced
Divorced
Survived (so far)

74

"...and if you look up, you will notice that this delightful family home still retains the original coving and picture rail features..."

HOST OF CELEBRITIES CHEER ROYAL PAIR ON

by BBC's Royal Correspondent **Jenny Flect**

A GLITTERING array of stars from the world of show-business were nowhere to be seen on Sophie and Edward's big day.

Instead, there was Sir David Frost, the host of TV's Sunday morning "Everyone's Still In Bed Show"; Screaming Lord Webber, composer and chairman of the Really Useless Group who first employed Edward as a Tea Bag Consultant; and E.R. Thatsit the Producer of "It's A Royal Cock-Up" in 1981.

That show was to be Edward's introduction to the glamorous business of tea-making (*Surely "entertainment"? Ed.*) and starred such famous people as Billy Connolly, John Travolta, Stuart Hall and the Duchess of York.

Sadly, none of them could make it to the wedding and amongst others who were not present either were Madonna, Tom Cruise, Monica Lewinsky, Hugh Grant, Mike Tyson, Gwyneth Paltrow, Tina Brown, Barbara Streisand, Sir Paul McCartney, Leonardo DiCaprio and Elvis Presley.

"Actually, madam, I can recommend everything"

Highlights From The TV Commentary

(What you missed while you were watching the Brookside Omnibus)

Sue Barking (*for it is she*): ...and there is the bride's mother, a commoner, and it would be hard to imagine anyone commoner than that...

Michael Buerking: Oh, come on, Sue, that's a bit unfair.

Sue Barking: Never can this former secretary have imagined that one day her daughter would find herself side-by-side with Sir David Frost and Andrew Lloyd Webber...

Michael Buerking: ...and isn't it a pleasure to see how informal and relaxed everyone is... and now a fanfare by the massed trumpeters of the Queen's Own Buglers Poursuivant dressed in their splendid livery.

Sue Barking: Yes, they're standing informally to attention in a lovely relaxed row awaiting Her Majesty the Queen...

Michael Buerking: Looking very relaxed... what a lovely touch, Sue, she's wearing a very relaxed hat.

Sue Barking: Yes, Michael, carrying a very informal handbag.

Michael Buerking: Probably the most informal handbag ever carried at a Royal Wedding...

Sue Barking: ...and what a relief that the rain has held off for this important day as the Duke of Edinburgh prepares to serve for the match.

Umpire: Quiet please.

(Continued Court 94)

Bumper Cars in the US

BLAIR BACK PEDDLES ON EURO

It's a EU-Turn

THE TORY PARTY
An Apology

IN recent years, in common with all other newspapers, we may have given the impression that the Conservative Party under Mr Hague would never have any hope of winning an election and was totally discredited as a force in British politics. Headlines such as "Is The Conservative Party Finished?", "Is Hague The Most Pathetic Party Leader Of All Time?" and "Resign, You Stupid Bald Squit", may have led readers to believe that we in some way thought that Mr Hague was failing to give the Tory Party the leadership necessary for it to regain any semblance of electability.

We now realise, after his historic triumph in the vital Euro-Elections, that the Conservatives are now an unstoppable political phenomenon, with the dynamism, vision, energy and commitment that will make their landslide victory at the next election inevitable. Furthermore, we accept that Mr Winston Hague is a statesman of unparalleled acumen whose inspired and courageous slogan "We want to be in Number 10 but not in Europe (although we are very much in favour of the EU)" so brilliantly spoke for the feelings of the 8 percent of the total electorate who bothered to walk down to their local school and vote.

We apologise unreservedly for any confusion this may have caused to our readers, and undertake not to repeat this grotesque misrepresentation of the truth until the next poll shows Labour on 64 percent and Mr Blair having an approval rating of 98 percent.

© All newspapers.

The Four Mr Men of the Apocalypse

I SEE EVIDENCE FOR WAR CRIMES
by John Pilger

Not in Kosovo, Tuesday

TODAY with my own eyes I saw incontrovertible evidence that NATO is guilty of the worst war crimes since America's genocide in Vietnam a quarter of a century ago.

The evidence was contained in several articles buried deep in the Guardian in which I, John Pilger, prove conclusively that it was NATO, not the Serbs who, on the orders of dictators Clinton and Blair, has secretly murdered millions of (cont. p. 94)

ANOTHER APOLOGY
KEVIN KEEGAN

IN COMMON with all other newspapers, we may have given the impression that we thought Kevin Keegan was in some way a footballing Messiah who would lead his country to victory. We now realise that Mr Keegan is, in fact, a turnip-head who
(That's enough apologies. Ed.)

Letter to the Editor

Brussels Busybodies

SIR – Surely there is no sound more redolent of everything that is best in Britain than the glorious whirring of our traditional British lawnmowers as they herald the coming of spring by roaring into action on a million lawns?

And are they now to be silenced for ever by some diktat from the power-crazed bureaucrats of Brussels? Are such ancient names in our island history as Suffolk Punch, Flymo, Atco and Honda to become the latest victims of these dictatorial busybodies?

We must preserve the noise of the countryside so that future generations will continue to enjoy the song of the strimmer and the cry of "I say, I wonder if you'd mind not mowing on Sunday afternoon. My wife and I are trying to enjoy a spot of quiet nooky." *(Surely "trying to do the Sunday Telegraph Prize Crossword"?)*

H. GUSSET
Dunmowin, Compo St Heap,
Dorset

"Sword of Truth...?"

FINAL HUMILIATION OF FORMER MINISTER

by Our Old Etonian Staff **Charles Moore** (O.E.)

THERE were heart-rending scenes in the heart of London's fashionable Westminster yesterday, when a team of bailiffs swooped on the £10 million luxury home of disgraced former Conservative Cabinet minister Jonathan Aitken, removing some of the ex-statesman's most precious possessions.

Those Possessions In Full

● 1 pair engraved cufflinks, the gift of His Royal Highness Sheikh Randi bin Shifti. *Estimated value £25,000*

● 1 signed photograph of the late President Nixon, inscribed "To Jonathan, the only guy who ever believed that I wasn't lying". *Estimated value £2*

● A selection of rare canes, formerly the property of "Miss Whippee – Norty Boys R Us". *Estimated value 10p*

● 1 wine glass, as emptied over the owner's head by TV-am's own Anna Ford. *Estimated value 25p*

● 10,000 items of personal memorabilia, including private letters from various aggrieved ladies, all ending "You bastard".

But the biggest blow of all for the man whom Mrs Thatcher once regarded as her natural successor was the bailiff's confiscation of his most prized possession of all – the jewel-encrusted "Sword of Truth", which hung over his drawing room mantelpiece, and which had been handed down to him as a cherished heirloom by his grandfather Lord Beavercrook.

A weeping Aitken told me, "They've not only taken the sword, but also the Trusty Shield of British Fairplay, which I had relied on to keep me out of prison.

"Now they have gone, I will have no alternative but to pay my debt to society, or rather not, since I have put the house in my wife's name."

The bailiffs, however, described the sword and shield as "worthless".

WHO'S WHO IN THE SENSATIONAL NEW STAR WARS MOVIE

The Eye's cut out and keep guide to the most talked about film in the last million years!

Anogud Skymovie — Jedi Princeling and future father of Luke Skysport.

Computa the Graffik — cuddly alien life form who befriends Jedi adviser, Ova the Hype.

Dearth of Ideaz — Dark Lord and servant of the evil Emperor Palpable-nonsense.

Princess Bora from the Planet ZZZZ — destined to marry Hans Christian Andersen in order to find plot.

NB-G2 — droid friend and accomplice of C5, the revolutionary Sinclair electric car that frees the universe from the evil JarJar-NotWarWar.

Queue Gon Home — Maverick Jedi warlord, brother of Obe Won-for servicestothe-theatre, and servant of Yawner, the Jedi guru.

(That's enough stupid characters from Star Bores. Ed.)

MONEY MATTERS

with Eye Moneyman **Gordon Brown**

Dear Gordon,
If you had 400 tons of gold, would you hang on to it or sell it?

GB writes:
The obvious thing to do is to hold on to it for a wee while. But not me! What I'm going to do is to announce in advance that I am going to sell it. This will make sure that its value drops by half. Canny, eh?

Dear Gordon,
What will you do with the money then?

GB writes:
The obvious thing to do would be to invest what remains in some strong currency like the dollar or the pound. But not me! I'm going to put it all in the euro, where it's bound to lose another half of its value. Canny, eh?

Dear Gordon,
Aren't you a bit of an idiot?

GB writes:
The obvious answer is yes.

© The Treasury

"No, listen... It's vital that we continue to pay the Danegeld to ensure that Britain retains her influence at the heart of ... er...Denmark"

England
999 A.D.

How I Kicked My Habit

by Tara Boomdiay-Tomkinson

IT IS now five minutes since I checked out of the internationally renowned centre for rehabilitation, The Quackery.

And, yes folks, I can confirm that it's true. Tara is no longer addicted to publicity.

I admit freely that I was an addict needing a daily fix of pictures and articles about myself. I became so desperate I was reduced to "doing" the Sunday Times.

My life was out of control. All I could think about was where I would get my next mention.

Friends were appalled. I would turn up looking terrible on the Frank Skinner Show, or in Tatler or even in Nigel Dempster's column.

But now, thanks to two weeks of therapy, counsellling and encounter sessions with other minor celebrities, I can proudly say that I no longer crave publicity.

That is why I am writing this column with a picture of me on top of it.
Tara Masalata-Tomkinson, The Sunday Timezzzzz.

Pre-School Nursery Facility Rhymes

Boys and girls come in from play,
The sun doth shine so bright today.
Leave your skipping and hide-&-seek
And revise for Key Stage 1 next week.

THE ALTERNATIVE VOICE

Dave Spart, Co-Chair of the Smash Capitalism and Windows Now Alliance *(a pro-anarchy organisation)*

ONCE again, a peaceful demonstration against world capitalism and monetary fascism has been hijacked by a small, violent group of organised militants, ie the police, who deliberately and sickeningly attempted to interfere with a totally non-confrontational protest of graffiti, arson and physical attacks on guilty employees of financial instititions... er... thus creating a so-called "riot" in central London which gave the police the excuse to close down the entire transport system of London, meaning innocent protestors, ie myself, could not get home on public transport and could not even get a cab due to shortage of cash thanks to the closure of the banks due to er... *(Cont. p. 94)*

THE RON DAVIES BOOK OF BIRD WATCHING

An Authoritative Guide to Britain's Woodland Wildlife

Thrush   Sparrow   Robin   Simon   Winston   Reporter from the News of The World

Heath's Private View

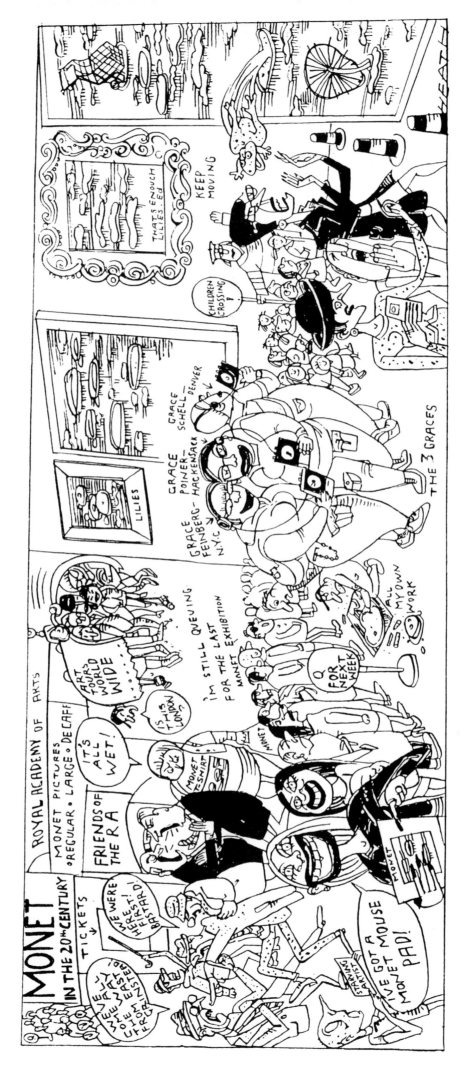

A MILLION POUNDS
UPFRONTERS

 At the Wedding of the Century — *only* Private Eye has the exclusive pictures of Posh 'n' Beck's Day to Remember!

♥ United at last! **Baby Spice** (left) kisses the **Posh** Bride. **Victoria** certainly picked a winner! "It's one **Beck** of a day!" says the groom (middle) as proud **Mum 'n' Dad Beckham** (right) watch him score!!

♥ It's a great Dane out for **Peter Schmeichel**! And who's that he's hoping to get between the Bed Posts? Why, it's **Sporty Spice**, of course, who's hoping he'll score! (*You've done that. Ed*)

♥ It's the **Adams Family**! **Posh** (middle) looking happy and **Victoria**-us while her proud Mum and Dad (left and right) wait to see the happy couple sent off! **Becksy** looks like he's going to score tonight! (*I said you've done this one. Ed*)

♥ **Ryan** looks like he's going to get the **Giggs**les with **Scary** on his arm! The Welsh dribbler must be hoping for an early bath this time! Maybe he'll score! (*You're fired. Ed*)

♥ Grin and **Behr** it, **Danni**! (Left) The TV presenter poses with someone from **Emmerdale** (check subs) and two of United's top players (poss **Skollager** and **Oranjeboom** — check). What a Flat Back Four! Surely one of them will score? (*You're hired again. Ed*)

GLENDA SLAGG

Fleet Street's Janet Street-Porter!

WHO do they think they are – David Beckham and his so-called wife Posh!?!?!?

Even the Royal Family aren't too grand to let the press have a peep at their moment of joy!?!?!?

Not so the Earl of Muckham and Princess Toffee-Nose – as they would no doubt like to be known???

"Keep Out!" That was their message to the gentlefolk of the press as they plighted their troth in bonnie Ireland!!

Well, here is Auntie Glenda's message to you – Get Stuffed!!

HATS off to the happy couple Posh and Becky for keeping their sacred day to themselves!!!

Not for them the greedy, grimy dirty mac brigade a-snoopin' and a-snappin' as they made their vows before God Almighty in his holy house!?!?

If only the Royals had shown the same respect for a private moment!! (Geddit?!?!?!)

THREE cheers and more for the Grand Old Lady of Royalty (The Queen Mother I'm talking about – stoopid!!?)

Just think of some of the sights this little old lady has seen in her long lifetime.

The sinking of the Titanic. The Battle of Waterloo. The Millennium Dome – to name only three.

Let's raise our glasses to the Greatest Granny of them all. Here's to ye, Ma'am – and long may you reign over us!?!?

THE Queen Mother – aren'tcha-sickofher!?!?! (No disrespect, Grandma!)

Every year the story is the same – the little old lady who's seen it all, from the sinking of the Titanic to the Battle of Waterloo!?!

For pity's sake, Ma'am, do us all a favour and put a right royal sock in it!!!

HERE THEY are, Glenda's scrumptious summer puddings:

● **SEAN CONNERY**. He may be bald, boring and bearded, but he's still got it where it counts – under his kilt!!! (Geddit?!?!)

● **DAMON HILL**. Okay, so he's given up racing, but he's certainly driving this gal round the bend and into the pits!!!

● **SIR SIMON RATTLE**. Forget Berlin – and come and *mis*-conduct yourself round my place. (Geddit!!?!?!)

Byeeee!!!!

"You may now kiss the groom"

The Daily Telegraph

A National Scandal

THIS newspaper has always set its face against the payment of large sums of money to the relatives of criminals, who seek to exploit for gain their connection with the perpetrators of malfeasance by selling their supposed "stories" to unscrupulous and unprincipled sections of the media.

It is easy to imagine the feelings of nausea and disgust which such transactions must excite in the hearts and minds of all right-thinking persons. Nevertheless, in certain circumstances, there may be a case for modest payments to be made by a newspaper to, say, the mother or daughter of, say, a former Cabinet minister who, through no fault of his own, has been hounded into prison.

There is a clear moral justification for making such payments where the victim of such injustice is, let us say, an Old Etonian.

© Charles Moore O.E.

On other pages

Exclusive: Nicola Horlick rings up Sarah Sands to tell her why she lost the Industrial Tribunal against her nanny because she didn't want to talk about her private life – and then talks about her private life at enormous length .... p. 2
Opinion: Sarah Sands on how ghastly and uppity nannies are getting nowadays .... p. 3
Fashion: What Nicola Horlick is wearing now that the nanny has (*That's enough. Ed.*)

The Most Moving Human Document You Will Ever Read

(exclusive to the Daily Aitkengraph)

The Ballad Of Belmarsh Gaol

A letter written by **Mr Jonathan Aitken** to his mother, **Mrs Ludmilla Aitken**

Private and Confidential
(Pass on to Charles Moore and tell him to put it in)

Dearest Mummy,

It is quite nice here and the other boys are all very nice. I have made friends with a black boy called Stokesy, who is very nice. I have helped him with his homework. Do you know, he cannot spell the word "Department of Social Security"? But otherwise he is very nice.

I am glad to say that the teachers (whom we have to call by their Christian names) are not too strict. Last night one of them let me watch "Question Time" on TV, which was very nice of him.

I have been going to chapel every day, and sometimes twice. I have said my prayers for you and the children and even Mr Rusbridger, who I am trying to learn to forgive even though he is a complete ****. In fact, some of the bigger boys here have said that when they get out, they wouldn't mind sorting him out for me.

The food is very nice. Today we had pasta and salad, with apple juice. Some of the other boys like smoking funny cigarettes which have a funny smell, but this is against the rules and you will be pleased to hear that I have not joined in! I am very keen to get my Merit Badge, which the headmaster (whom we call "the Governor") has said would allow me to come home in just a few months. He is very nice (the Governor, I mean) and I am really enjoying my first term here.

I miss you and my Rolex watch very much.

Your loving son,
Jonathan.

P.S. Can you please *not* send me the tuck from Fortnum's that you promised, as it would only make the other chaps jealous and they might begin to rag me for being a snob.

The Alternative Rocky Horror Service Book

No 94: A Service Of Blessing For The Toddlers Of Non-Churchgoing Or Agnostic Parents

President (*for it is she*):	A very warm welcome to you all!
All:	Thanks.
President:	And whose little kiddy is this?
The Parents Of The Child:	It is ours, or at least it's hers by her previous partner (*or it may be his by his previous partner of either sex*).
President:	Isn't he or she sweet?
The Congregation:	Aaaah! (*or they may say Ooooh!*)
President:	Great!

(*Here may be played a suitable piece of recorded devotional music. It may be "Candle in the Wind" by Sir Elton John, or the Theme from the The Teletubbies Christmas Video*)

THE ADDRESS

President:	We are not gathered together in the sight of God, because that's not the point of this very special day for little N or M (here he may name the child, as it may be Wain or Shasni). We are not here to stuff a lot of old-fashioned propaganda down people's throats, going on about Jesus, the devil and all that stuff. We're not here to be judgemental. We're here to have a nice occasion and hope that in years to come N or M may remember today and think it might be quite nice to pop into a church from time to time and see what it's all about.
Congregation:	Is that it?
President:	Well, actually, we usually have a hymn here. But you've probably got better things to do than stand around in church waiting for your baby to be blessed.
All:	Get on with it!

THE ACT OF BLESSING

President:	Bless you!
Congregation:	Take care!
President:	Be lucky!
Congregation:	Cheers!

(*All shall then process to the home of the infant, where a party will keep the neighbours awake until 3 o'clock in the morning*)

"*It's amazing what you can do with one hair*"

Friday, July 9, 1999

DIRTY DIGGER MARRIES GOLD-DIGGER

EXCLUSIVE HONEYMOON PIX

The royal couple

by Our Invasion Of Privacy Staff **TERRY PHOTO-LENS**

COR!! What a lovely pair! And Rupert and Wendy look nice too! Blimey! Wicked Wendy (32,24,32) can't wait to get her hands on his assets! And Randy Rupert ($52 Billion) can't wait to get down to business with her! Fancy a Peking Duck, Wendy? Or is Rupert going to show you his hundred-year-old eggs?

VULGAR RUBBISH

Forget the pictures of Sophie's Tit, look at Wendy's *(He's the old bloke on the right!?)* OK, so we faked the photo! Sorry, Rupe, it was all in good clean fun. Hope you don't take offence, cobber, or we'll buy up your ex-wife's story!? Get the picture?! We didn't, but we put one in anyway!?

THE SUN SAYS

HAS she got a currant bun in the oven?

We have a right to know.

SHOULD VOTE HUNTING BE BANNED?

by Our Political Staff
Charles James Fox

THERE were renewed calls last night for an immediate countrywide ban on the hunting of votes.

Objectors described appalling recent scenes in which the Prime Minister dressed himself up in red and indulged in a sickening and cold-blooded chase of votes.

"It made my stomach turn," said one protester. "Blair seemed to get a real kick out of it. He and his upper-class cronies got together and rode roughshod over the entire countryside before going in for the kill."

However Mr Blair, who is Master of the Islington Hunt, defended what he called "an essential feature of traditional English life".

STUPID HUNT

"All we are doing," he said, "is trying to keep the votes under control. You can't have votes roaming around threatening our livelihoods."

He continued: "Besides, I present a wonderful spectacle as I charge around at the head of my traditional followers, with our whips working overtime and our timeless cries of 'Tally Votes!' and 'Left-Wing View Hulloo!' "

TV Highlights

Prescott And Son

BBC1 9.00pm *(Repeat)*

IN tonight's episode of the classic comedy, the upwardly-mobile John (played by Harold Steptoe) is mocked by his father Bert (played by Albert Steptoe) for betraying his working class roots and mixing with "the middle classes".

Young John is mortified and tells his father to mind his own business. "I'll never speak to you again, you dirty old booger," he tells the old man before he opens a bottle of champagne and eats a bucket of caviar.
Eye Rating: Hilarious.

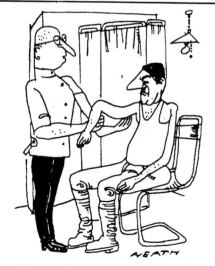

"It's repetitive strain injury mein Führer"

ROYAL WEDDING SOUVENIR

To celebrate the union of the Earl of Sex and his new bride, the Countess of Deng, now you too can acquire this exquisite hand-crafted Satellite Dish lovingly fashioned by nine-year-old children in the legendary sweatshops of Guandong.

IN YEARS to come your Heritage Dish will not only become a priceless heirloom for your children to cherish, but it can also be used to beam in the world's finest Chinese satellite TV programmes, including *Great Wall Journeys*, *Tibetan Neighbours From Hell*, *Dr Who Chi Minh* and *Chinese Dentists Go Bonking* (adults only).

For only £99.99 (plus monthly payments of £12.99) this priceless dish will be delivered to your home within 28 days.

WARNING: dishes may come without a picture of the happy couple but may carry instead the BSkyB logo.

It's The Wedding Of The Century-Old-Man

IS THE SUN GOOD FOR YOU AFTER ALL?

by Our Medical Staff **Dr James Lefuwotascorcha**

SCIENTISTS have always believed that the Sun was extremely damaging to anyone exposed to it, but sensational new research suggests that, in fact, the Sun can be beneficial to health if taken in moderate doses.

The survey, published by top medical research laboratories based in Wapping, claims that the Sun does not, as previously thought, turn your brain into jelly within minutes, causing irritation, nausea and death through terminal boredom.

On the contrary, says Professor Murdoch, the Sun makes you feel better by "giving you a laugh, relaxing the muscles of your brain, and improving my circulation".

Sun Blockhead

Said one of the patients in the survey, a Mr Tony B. from Downing Street: "I always used to try to keep out of the Sun. But now I'm in it all the time – and I've never felt better. Every day I get less and less red. In fact I'm not even slightly pink."

Top spin doctors are backing the report, saying there is no such thing as "over exposure". Said Dr Alastair Campbell: "You don't even have to cover up. Just lie in the Sun and you'll be fine."

That Murdoch/Deng Wedding Breakfast In Full

No. 13 *Porn Crackers*

No. 25 *Steamy Nudells*

No. 34 *Dim Sun Owner*

No. 42 *Egg Fu Wotascorcha*

No. 69 *Fortune Hunting Cookie*

To Follow

No. 94 *Viagra Fritters*

END OF WORLD FAILS TO ARRIVE SHOCK

Old French Bore Proved Wrong

MILLIONS of people all over the world were deeply disappointed last night when the long-promised end of the world failed to materialise.

Hundreds of thousands stayed up specially to see the apocalypse on Sky TV, but were furious when all they saw was a repeat of a 1963 episode of Z-Cars starring Brian Blessed and Stratford Johns.

Experts had rested their hopes for an Armageddon-style conflagration on some verses published in 1559 by the French soothsayer Nostradamus.

The key passage in which the end of the world was predicted in exact detail came in the 21st stanza of the 14th canto of his immortal work:

"Then shall there be strange portents in the seventh month
When thousands shall form lines in a street in France
Waiting for the Man of Straw to give them paper.[1]

And, lo, a saintly woman shall ride forth
With soup, to give them succour in their dire plight.[2]
While on Thames-side a strange harridan
With raucous voice and jutting teeth
Will become the Queen of the Indies.[3]

Then shall it be clear that ye Ende is nigh for all life as we knowe it.

Make ye no mistake.[4]

1. Nostradamus here clearly foresaw the difficulties faced by the British Passport Agency in Petty France in getting their computers to work.

2. Clearly a reference to the intervention of the Shadow Home Secretary Anne Widdecombe.

3. Clearly Nostradamus was here referring to the sensational appointment of Janet Street-Porter as editor of the Sunday Independent.

4. Clearly a reference to the end of the world which was at the last minute cancelled due to lack of interest.

ALL YOU CAN KEEP DOWN £3

THAT NEW LABOUR INTEGRATED TRANSPORT POLICY IN FULL

1. Public transport is overcrowded, unreliable, under-funded and close to breakdown.
2. Every means must be employed to encourage people to use public transport rather than their cars.
3. er...
4. Private Helicopter Lanes on all motorways for use by public officials such as John Prescott.
5. er...
6. That's it.

The Railtrack Children

NEW CAPTAIN FOR TITANIC

by Our Sinking Staff **Stephen Glugger**

IT was a night to remember last night when the owners of the Sunday Titanic made a controversial appointment, hiring a new captain to command their famous flagship in mid-voyage.

She is Janet Street-Porter, a former celebrity, who replaces Captain Kim Fletcher as from today.

Said the vessel's proprietor, Mr Simon Kellner, "Ms Street-Porter will make a fantastic captain. She has no experience of ocean-going liners, nor any record of achievement in navigation or seamanship. I have, however, seen her on the television and I once met her in the Groucho Club. So she seems the obvious candidate for the job."

HELLO FAILURE
(Surely "sailor"? Ed.)

Ms Street-Porter outlined her plans for the Sunday Titanic's "maiden" voyage in a meeting with the entire 15-strong crew. "It's time this ship appealed to different passengers. So, from now on it'll be women and children first," she told them. "My idea is for the Titanic to get cool, right? And you don't get much cooler than an iceberg, ok? Chill out!"

John F. Kennedy Junior – An Apology

IN COMMON with all other newspapers, we heard the news about Kennedy a bit on the late side yesterday and cobbled together twenty pages saying Kennedy was a national hero, the true heir to Camelot, whose death would be mourned by the entire American nation.

Headlines such as "Americans Weep For Their Diana", "Last of the Golden Dynasty Taken From Us", and "The Tragedy To End All Tragedies" may have given the impression that we regarded the late Mr Kennedy as a national icon, the only hope for his generation, and a shining beacon for the entire civilised world.

We now realise that there was not a jot or scintilla of truth in this whatsoever, and that the young John Kennedy was nothing more than a pampered playboy whose reckless self-indulgence led inevitably to not only his own premature death but to that of his wife and sister-in-law.

We would like to apologise to all our readers for any confusion this may have caused.

CURSE OF THE KENNEDYS

by Our Kennedy Staff **Nigel** (formerly known as Dempster)

IT SEEMS like some terrible curse. Just when things appear to be going well and the future looks bright, another Kennedy dies and everyone is obliged to read through hundreds of articles about the curse of the Kennedys.

It all began with JFK, but every few years history repeats itself with uncanny regularity: Chappaquiddick, the skiing accident, the one after that, Bobby Kennedy (or was that before?) ... er... er... the grassy knoll, er... er... er... will this do?

© All newspapers. First printed in 1963.

That Doomed Kennedy Clan

Sir Ludovic Kennedy	=	Lady Euthanasia Kennedy

| Charles Kennedy (doomed Liberal Democrat leader) | Nigel Kennedy (ill-fated violinist, shot by an angry music lover) | Red Kennedy (doomed London Mayor eaten alive by his own newts) | Sarah Kennedy (ill-fated Radio 2 disc jockey with alcohol problems) | John F. Kennedy Airport (doomed air terminal where millions of suitcases mysteriously disappear every year) |

"Mummy said her first word to me today, Nanny"

NEW LEADER DENOUNCES 'ERRORS OF BIRTISM'

Former Great Helsman Chose 'Wrong Path'

IN A five-hour speech delivered before thousands of cheering BBC workers in the Great Hall of Broadcasting House, the newly elected Director-General of the BBC, Mr Gregori Dykov, made a savage attack on his predecessor, the now-discredited Comrade Birtsky.

The former DG was described as a "faceless authoritarian, obsessed with bureaucracy" who had taken the organisation "down the wrong road" with "his five-year plans and his love of jargon and committees".

"For too many years," Dykov went on, "the whole organisation was drowning in a sea of memorandums and meaningless paperwork."

Capitalist Running D-G

"Morale among the workers has been reduced to zero. From all over the country we have had delegations from discontented corporation activists, imploring us to end the catastrophe of Birtism."

After half-an-hour of prolonged applause, Mr Dykov concluded, "Birtsky is exposed as a collaborator with the international digitalist conspiracy which is seeking the overthrow of all public service broadcasting as we know it.

"Furthermore, he and his wife Birtskova, have for years been feathering their own nests with inflated salaries, four-wheel drive vehicles and Armani suits, at the expense of the downtrodden masses."

Birts Of A Feather

"His grandoise building schemes in White City have become the laughing stock of the civilised world.

"Today they stand as mute testaments to his overweaning ambition and megalomania."

To renewed cheering, Comrade Dykov pledged "a return to the old values which made the BBC the envy of all mankind, with programmes such as Dad's Army, Housewives' Choice and Dick Barton, Special Agent."

Only Fools And Husseys

As Comrade Dykov concluded his oration, there was a rush to the podium by former senior Birtists, vying with one another to heap scorn on the policies of their one-time Dalek-General.

Said Comrade Yentob-ovitch, "I never believed in Birtism. Many a time I pleaded with him for a return to quality pro-gramming, but he would not listen.

"He just smiled and ordered even more repeats of Noel's House Party and The National Lottery Show."

Also outspoken in his condemnation of the former regime was another senior apparatchik who owed his career to Birtsky, Comrade Bannisterov, the hated Head of Radio.

"We constantly plotted his downfall, but he was too clever for us, always offering us more money and better jobs."

Then Comrade Boylov spoke up (cont'd. p. 94)

Wimbledon Highlights – What You Missed

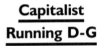 Semi-Final

Kissinger H. (US) v. Paxman J. (GB)

IN what was perhaps the most exciting match the BBC has ever covered, two of the all-time Titans of the game clashed in a fight to the death which had the BBC Centre Court crowd gasping in horror.

The highly-fancied British boy Tim Paxman opened with a dazzling serve: "You're just a fat mass-murderer, aren't you?"

The American was clearly caught on the wrong foot: "Er, isn't that a bit rude?" he volleyed back.

Paxman went in for the kill: "Shouldn't you be put on trial for war crimes?" he thundered.

The German-born US veteran could only flail wildly: "Do you realise who I am?" he countered.

But Paxman then went in for a final cheap shot, with the crowd roaring "Paxman! Paxman!": "You're worse than Hitler, aren't you, four-eyes?"

Kissinger was lost for a reply and stormed off the court, saying that he would order B-52s round to bomb Paxman's luxury £2 million Rumpole-style Oxfordshire hideaway.

At this point, the match was therefore abandoned. In a post-match interview Kissinger blamed his coach: "I was assured that it was a friendly game, and that Paxman would just lob easy ones at me like 'What is the title and price of your brilliant new book?'"

Dr Strangelove is 89.

POETRY CORNER

**In Memoriam
Stanley Kubrick
(1931-2001)**

So. Farewell then
Stanley Kubrick
Famous film director
And
Inventor of
The Cube.

2001 Dalmatians —
That was your best-known
Film.

Everyone remembers the
Beginning.

Boom-boom-boom-boom-
Boom.
Dum... dum... DA-DA!!!!

Brilliant!

Unfortunately I cannot
Remember
The rest of
The film.

> E.J.Thribb (17½)

**In Memoriam
Ted Hughes**

So. Hullo again.
Ted Hughes.

Now that you are dead
You are winning
More prizes
Than
Ever before.

First the T.S. Eliot.
Then the
Whitbread.

What next?
Perhaps they will make you
Poet Laureate.
> The late E.J. Thribb (17½)

E.J. Thribb will be reading
from a collection of his life's
work *Better Dead Than Read* at
Waterstone's Bookshop,
Neasden High Street, on
Tuesday morning at 9.30am.

POETRY CORNER

**In Memoriam
Lord "Lew" Grade,
TV Mogul and Winner of
the 1926 World
Charleston Competition**

So. Farewell then
Lord Grade.

With your bulky frame
And large cigar
You epitomised
The world of showbusiness.

It was you who gave us
The Saint, Crossroads and
The Muppet Show.

Now you have reached
Life's Crossroads
And you may become a
Saint.

(Or perhaps a
Muppet.)

E.J. Kermit the Thribb (17½)

**In Memoriam: Lines
Written On The Death Of
Japanese Cinematic Giant
Akira Kurosawa**

Ah so. Farewell then
Akira Kurosawa.

Or should I say
Sayonara?

You were the director of
The Magnificent Seven
Samurai,
Which was a brilliant
Film

Starring Yul Brynner,
Steve McQueen,
Charles Bronson and Eli
Wallach.

Da, da, da, da
Da-da-da-da-da.

That was your
Theme tune.

Although it is hard to
Convey it
In a poem.

E.J. Thribb (Magnificent 17½)

Letters to the Editor

The Sad Demise of English Cricket

SIR – There can be no doubt as to what lies behind our recent humiliating defeat at the hands of the New Zealanders.

Not so long ago the sight of small boys playing with bat and ball and a crude wicket chalked up on the wall was familiar to us all.

The cries of "Howzat" echoed across city street and village lane. It is no wonder that we produced such greats as F.J. Plard, Sir Wilfred Pugwash and, more recently, Nottingham-shire's Ian Snote.

But now, thanks to out-of-town supermarkets, there are no playing fields on which our youngsters can hone their skills with willow and leather.

Only when the government outlaws traffic on Britain's streets can we hope to retain our rightful position as the world's greatest cricketing nation.

REV. C.J. BARKWORTH,
The Knights Templar
Retirement Home,
Malta.

SIR – There can be no doubt that if there is one single factor behind the collapse of our beloved national game of cricket it is the fear amongst the general public of the omni-present paedophile.

There was a time when small boys felt free to take off their jerseys and use them as wickets without some evil paedophile lurking behind a tree.

But now, thanks to the inaction of the police force and the laissez-faire Sixties morality of successive governments, no boy dares play cricket in public – with the lamentable results we have seen this summer.

COLONEL L.B.W.
BONKERS,
The Long Room,
Hutton St Leonard,
Dorset.

SIR – Surely there is a simple explanation as to why Messrs Hussein, Atherton, Ramprakash et al lost the series against New Zealand. It is because they were no good!

DAVE BLIMEY,
via e-mail.

SIR – There is nothing new in the present sad plight of the England Cricket XI. One only has to go back to the summer of 1837 when the national side under Captain Major Wilber-force Farrah-Hockley failed to score a single run in five test matches against the visiting team from the Pitcairn Islands. Yet, in the following year under their new captain, the Maharajah of Vindaloo, England defeated what was possibly the strongest cricket team ever fielded by Tibet by a margin of three games to two – and all this despite bowling figures of 6-984 by the Dalai Lama!

So, let the England selectors take heart. We may have lost the battle but it is always darkest before the dawn!

SIR REGINALD TRUSSET,
"Maidenover",
Batting Average,
Somerset.

That Parkinson Honorary Degree From Hull University In Full

SALUTAMUS MICHAELUM PARKINSONIUS, NOMINATES VULGARE "PARKY", FILIUS BARNSLEYENSIS ET HOSPES CHATTERATUS PROGRAMMIS IN TELEVISIONE PER MULTOS ANNOS SYCOPHANTISSIMIS AD CELEBEBRITATIS AMERICANOS, PER EXEMPLO CASSIUS CLAYIUS ET FREDERICUS ASTAIRUS ET BOBBUS HOPUS ET CETERA ET CETERA. SED MEMORABILIS SUPER OMNES PER INCIDENTUM QUANDO HUMILIATUS ERAT AB EMU, AVIS HORRIBILIS AUSTRALIS, ET MANIPULATOR RODERICUS HULLIUS, AD TREMENDISSIMO DILECTIUM OMNE POPULI, QUI CONTINUERUNT DISCUSSERE HIC MOMENTUS IN HISTORIA TELEVISUALIS BRITANNICI AD INFINITUM. SALUTAMUS EMU, AUT DOCTORUS EMU, HONORARIUM PROFESSORE LITTERAE. *(CERTE SHUMUS ERRORUS? EDITORIUS)*

© UNIVERSITY OF ROD HULL MXCIX

KNACKER – NEW DANDO THEORY

by Our Crime Staff **Nick Blackman**

A PLAINLY-delighted Inspector Knacker of the Yard revealed to a crowded press conference today that Jill Dando's killer was "almost certainly" an extraterrestrial being.

Said the Inspector, "We have examined minute markings on the pavement which match the patterns made by spacecraft leaving in a hurry."

Knacker continued, "This is why we have never been able to arrest the alien hitman who may well have had an obsession with the popular TV presenter and become infuriated when his advances were rejected."

NO IDEAS AT ALL

But this was not all the Inspector revealed to amazed journalists.

"The alien hitman theory is only one of thousands of leads which we are following up in the hope of convincing the public that we do have a clue what happened here."

"They don't really know what they're saying – they just mimic sounds they've heard!"

SHOULD LIB DEMS BE LEGALIZED?

by Our Medical Staff **Dr Thomas Splifferford**

A FIERCE debate was re-opened last night over the question of whether the Liberal Democrat Party should become freely available to the general public.

Said spokesman Charles Kennedy, "Thousands of people have experimented with Liberal Democracy at some stage of their lives, but few of them have become addicted."

GRASS ROOTS

He continued, "Many young people secretly try out the odd Liberal Democrat Policy but then as they get older they give it up."

However, opponents of the "Legalise Kennedy" campaign were quick to point out the dangers of allowing a third "hallucinogenic political party" to be legalised.

Said one critic, "We already have two dangerous parties on the market – Labour and Conservative. Are we seriously suggesting that we want a third? Especially when so little is known about the effects of it?"

GOING TO POT

He concluded, "Other countries have introduced Liberal Democracy with fatal results. They sit around in a dazed state talking nonsense about changing the world and living in peace and harmony."

Charles Kannabis is 24.

NEW RACING SCANDAL

What do you fancy in the 4 o'clock?

Your missus

AMAZING NEW EVIDENCE THAT CHIMPS CAN COMMUNICATE

by Our Science Staff **Lunchtime O'Rangutan**

TODAY I saw with my own eyes that a group of monkeys equipped with keyboards can produce a daily newspaper.

When I visited the Wapping compound of the Murdoch Research Institute, I witnessed a sight I shall never forget.

One fully grown-up ape, affectionately known to his keeper as "Yelland", was shown a photograph of holidaymakers sitting on the beach.

Within minutes he had tapped out on his keypad the sentence "Phew What A Scorcher – Britain Sizzles In Mediterranean-Style Heatwave".

One of his fellow-chimps was then shown a picture of a semi-clad girl from Essex.

Again, within a short time, he keyed in the words "Phew What A Stunna – Britain Sizzles As Tracy Strips Off".

A third picture was then presented to the chimps, showing media-mogul Rupert Murdoch.

Garry is almost human and is so clever that he can switch on Sky TV unaided!

At this they became restless and excited, and tried to lick the bottom of the man in the photograph.

Said one supervisor, "These apes are really showing remarkable progress, but it is early days and it will be some years before we can let them loose to run The Times."

HOW THE WORLD SAW THE GREATEST
  EVENT OF THE MILLENNIUM

11.37am How it looked in Frankfurt, as bankers left their VDU screens to witness the once-in-a-lifetime spectacle.

11.57am Romanians packed the streets of Bucharest as the sky went black.

12.26pm What millions of Iranians were allowed out of prison to see in Tehran.

2.12pm Fishermen in the Bay of Bengal gasped in amazement as the world went dark.

6.24am Detroit: millions of Americans were disappointed when the sun failed to disappear.

Post-Eclipse Depression Syndrome (PEDS)

Dr Thomas Stuttaford

Medical Briefing

IN THE wake of last week's eclipse many people will have experienced PEDS, as we doctors call it. What happens is that, after becoming unnaturally excited for several days in expectation of seeing something out of the ordinary, the patient becomes confused and bewildered when nothing of the kind occurs. At first he experiences the Anger Phase, when he lashes out at the Daily Telegraph for having promised that he would see amazing flashing lights and penumbras at the moment of the sun's disappearance, none of which materialised. He then enters the Depression Phase, where he compulsively repeats "If you ask me, it was a non-event" to anyone who will listen. He then goes into the Frustration Phase when he reads the newspapers the following day, only to discover that he has clearly missed out on an amazing experience which he can never hope to enjoy again unless he lives to the age of 129.

APOLOGY
The Eclipse

IN RECENT months, in common with all other papers, we may have given the impression that the recent solar eclipse was going to be a uniquely dramatic spectacle, providing an experience that none of us would ever forget. Headlines such as "The Greatest Show On Earth", "Stand By For The Greatest Natural Event Of All Time" and "Whatever You Do, Don't Look At It Or Your Eyes Will Be Permanently Damaged" could well have led readers to suppose that they should drop everything (except of course their special safety glasses) to see the world plunged into an apocalyptic darkness which would lead cows to run amok in fields, dogs to bark uncontrollably, and thousands of motorists to collide with each other in multiple pile-ups.

We now accept that there was not a jot or scintilla of truth in these prognostications, and we are happy to make it clear that the so-called eclipse was a "non-event" largely got up by the press to sell newspapers. So, far from seeing any of the above phenomena, members of the public might have concluded that they were in the presence of nothing more spectacular than a wet Sunday afternoon in Wolverhampton in November.

ECLIPSE BLACKS OUT NEWS
by Our Eclipse Staff **Phil Space**

THE whole country was kept in complete darkness for several days about what was happening in the world when a solar eclipse completely covered every newspaper in the country.

People put on special spectacles to try and find a story about Northern Ireland, Kosovo or the Prince of Wales going swimming – but to no avail.

"I think I have gone blind," said one reader. "I keep looking at the pages and all I can see is a huge blobby circle with the words 'Total Eclipse' written underneath it."

"Hi, it's me — just ringing to say I won't be home on the 6.10..."

BEST EVER EXAM RESULTS

Blunkett Denies Dumbing Down Charge

by Our Education Staff **GCSE Pass**

IN a move to counter allegations that the GCSE examinations had been made easier to secure a greater number of passes, the education secretary today released a specimen paper to show that the standard was "as high as ever, if not higher".

GCSE Maths Multiple Choice

You may use a calculator or ask your teacher the answers.

❶ Fill in the missing number from this sequence: 1, 2, 3, 4, —, 6, 7

Is it: **a)** 5
b) 217
c) Oasis Greatest Hits.

❷ Look closely at this week's winning Lottery numbers. If they are the same as yours, you won't ever have to worry about exams again.

Time allowed: 2 years

ANNOUNCEMENT

THERE are still some places available for students on the following courses:

AROMATHERAPY (with Crop Circle Studies),
Neasden University (formerly Brent Cross Polytechnic)

BATMAN STUDIES (with French),
The University of the Trossachs
(formerly Glenmiller Academy)

CULINARY MAINTENANCE AND MODERN GREEK,
University of Canvey (formerly The South End
Institute of Catering)

DIANA STUDIES (with Frisbee),
University of Chelsea (formerly The Harbour Club)

EXOTIC SUBSTANCES AND YODELLING,
University of Yeovil (formerly Paddy Ashdown Polytechnic)

Minimum Entry Grades: 2 Fs.

YARDIES RESPONSIBLE FOR CRIME WAVE

by Our Crime Staff **Nick Nobody**

A GROUP of corrupt and drug-crazed villains are behind London's spiralling lawlessness, according to new evidence destroyed last night.

The so-called "Scotland Yardies" operate in gangs and are easily recognisable by their distinctive blue clothes, traditional pointed headgear and habit of driving around making a lot of noise.

They are notoriously incompetent and *(cont. p. 94)*

"Send Travellers Home" say locals

by Our Go Home Affair Staff **Barry Fantoniblair**

THERE WERE angry calls last night for a family of immigrants to be repatriated immediately, after they had swamped a Tuscan Palazzo with their assorted children and hangers-on.

The Blairs had been living in housing paid for by local taxpayers since their arrival.

"They are just spongers" said local spokesman Giacomo Strani. "They come over here supposedly seeking 'sanctuary' and what do they do? Strut around as if they own the place and abuse our hospitality."

BEYOND THE PALIO

However, it seems that the protestors have succeeded at least partially in their demands, since the travellers have moved on to Southern France where they are squatting in an agreeable villa belonging to someone else.

Ten Ways To Keep Your Kids Safe And Happy This Summer

1. Do not let your children talk to anyone except an authorised adult such as the Head of Ofsted.
2. Do not let your children go out of doors at any time.
3. Lock them up for a minimum of 24 hours a day.
4. Do not let any stranger within a mile of your home.
5. Encourage your children to engage in activities that do not involve dangerous human contact – watching television, surfing the internet or playing video games.
6. Er…
7. You know it makes sense.
8. Er…
9. Er…
10. That's it.

(Issued by the NSPCC – the National Society for the Prevention of Carefree Children)

OMAGH REMEMBERED

"We are going to hunt down the bombers..."

"... so that we can offer them police protection"

STONE CLAD THE WINTER PALACE NOW

NOEL EDMONDS FOR TSAR

SATELLITE TV FOR ALL

RGJ

"Frankly I expected the revolution of the proletariat to be more dramatic"

General Pinochet Interviews Dominic Lawson

IT IS HARD to imagine that the quiet bespectacled figure sitting in front of me in his Sussex mansion is regarded as one of the ruthless figures ever to preside over a Sunday newspaper.

In a frank and fearless interview I put the following question to the hated tyrant:

"Dominic, you have a reputation for being a dictator whose regime carried out terrible purges where your readers mysteriously disappeared. Can you tell me aaaargh... !!!"

THE TOP 100 FILMS OF THE MILLENNIUM

IN the largest poll of cinema critics ever conducted, 10,000 of the world's top movie experts have drawn up the definitive list of the 100 best films ever made.

1 SAYONARA (1947). Toyota's masterpiece telling of a samurai warrior's unrequited love for a geisha. (219 minutes)

2 LES QUATRE CENTS DALMATIENS (1959). Jean-Paul Renault's masterpiece set in a 19th century Normandie chateau where a group of people gather on the eve of the Franco-Prussian war. (307 mins)

3 GOLDEN SYRUP (1958). Hjalmar Volvo's masterpiece set in 12th century Finland centres on a dialogue between the abbot of Helsingfors monastery and the figure of Death. (418 mins)

4 GROZNY (1936). Nikolai Moskovitch's 12-part Soviet Realist masterpiece set in the Russia of Ivan The Terrible, seen through the eyes of a brave young peasant boy with classic score by Igor Sonovabitch. (219 hrs)

5 MIRACOLO DI ROMA (1948). Federico Ferrari's masterpiece tells the touching story of a young boy's wartime friendship with a monkey. (2 hrs)

6 GOODBYE MR KIPLING (1947). Austin Cambridge's boarding-school masterpiece set in the fictional St Cakes, set on the eve of the First World War. Unforgettable performances from Alistair Sim, Robert Donat and the young David Tomlinson as Morris Minor. (121 mins)

7 STRIKE! (1938). Henry Ford's depression masterpiece recreates the great 1937 cotton-workers strike seen through the eyes of a young girl. (385 mins)

Andrej Lada's Macbeth (1961) set in 19th century Warsaw (never released)

8 KALI WALLAH (1951) Ray Hatterjee's masterpiece evoking the Bombay of his childhood. (312 mins)

(That's enough films. Ed.)

"Bernard's preparing for the Millennium"

THE MAJOR MEMOIRS

In what is being hailed by its publishers Harper-Collins as "the greatest political document of the millennium," former Prime Minister John Major looks back on his tumultuous seven years at the pinnacle of power.

NOW READ ON:

MR HANLEY — "useless"   MR CLARKE — "let me down"   MR HURD — "toffee-nosed snob"

WHEN SIR Robin Butler rang me up to say that I had become prime minister, I had little idea of how difficult the job was to turn out to be. Oh no.

This was in no small measure due to a certain woman, who made my life a hell on earth from day one. And I am not referring to my wife Norman! She was always supportive except on the frequent occasions when she was otherwise engaged in promoting her new career as an author and celebrity in her own right!

The woman to whom I refer was of course my predecessor Mrs Thatcher, who was to remain a not inconsiderable thorn in my flesh throughout the seven years of my premiership.

I do not in any way wish to rake up old wounds. In my judgement it is always better to draw a line in the sand under such matters.

Nevertheless, it is only fair to say that, without her constant interference, I would still be in Number 10 today.

ANOTHER person who let me down very badly indeed was John Redwood when I resigned as prime minister to allow anyone who wished to challenge my way of doing things to stand up and be counted.

It was unforgiveable of Mr Redwood to dare to stand against me.

Once again, I have no desire to dig up old sores, or to call him names. But in my book Mr Redwood is a BASTARD and as such I bought a special exercise book from Ryman's to put his name in. I called it my Bastard Book and I have it before me as I write these very words. Oh yes.

Here are some other names in the book:
Mr Lamont
Mr Waldegrave
Mrs Bottomley
Mr Howard
Mr Rifkind
not to mention everybody else in my Cabinet.

I think it is fair to say that, without their constant disloyalty, I would still be enjoying the fruits of office to this day.

ANOTHER big problem was all the Conservative MPs, who spent their entire time trying to make me look silly. For instance, when I had my very good idea for setting up a Cones Hotline, all they did was laugh.

This gave the impression that our Party was divided, and that I did not have the powers of leadership to hold it together.

This was quite untrue, and I think it is fair to say that if the MPs had shown more loyalty, I might still be occupying the position which is unfortunately held by Mr Blair.

The MPs were not the only people to let me down. Right from the start, the newspapers tried to portray me as just a boring little man in glasses and a grey suit. As anyone who has read these memoirs will by now have realised, this is a travesty of the true John Major, who in my judgement would still be prime minister today if it was not for those bastards in the media.

Tomorrow: How my brother Terry helped to make me look an idiot with his silly book of memoirs, which I never read because it was totally inaccurate, eg. on p. 361, where he states that the second bike I got for Christmas was a Hercules Kestrel, when as the photograph on p. 52 clearly showed, it was a Raleigh Roadmaster. I hope future historians will not regard Terry's book as in any way a reliable source. I hope they will also recognise that if it had not been for Terry's cheap publicity-seeking antics, I would almost certainly have won the 1997 election by a landslide, and Mr Hague would have remained a complete nobody, which is what he is, although as a former leader of the Conservative Party, I naturally wish him well.

FRENCH JUDGE BRIBED BY DUKE OF EDINBURGH

by Mirror Reporter **Pierre Moron**

THE FRENCH judge investigating the death of the late Princess Diana accepted a massive bribe of £200 million, according to sources close to Harrods Boss Mohammed Fayed.

The Duke's aim apparently was to cover up the real facts of her death, ie that she was murdered by the SAS disguised as MI5 photographers using a nuclear-powered Fiat Uno with James Bond-style laser headlights that vanished into outer space following the fatal gamma ray execution of the Princess.

COMPLETE RUBBISH

As a result of the Duke's bung, say sources, the judge came up with a ludicrous theory that the accident occurred because the car's driver had been drunk and the passengers had not been wearing seat-belts.

THE TIMES

Libby Purves

SHE's fat, she's feisty, she's fun and she's fifty. And she doesn't give a damn about clothes or make-up. She tells the truth as it is. And she makes the men around her look pathetic. I say hats off to myself, I mean, Ann Widdecombe *(cont'd. p. 94)*

WHATDOYOUDO
WHATDOYOUDO
WHATDOYOUDO
WHATDOYOUDO

Owl Drinks Party

93

Blond Youth Wears Sunglasses

by Our Entire Staff **Phil Space**

A tall young man, aged 17, yesterday put on a pair of sunglasses. *(Reuter)*

Inside:

And much, much more... Remember, it's always the Willy Season in the Daily Willograph

94

Letters to the Editor

The Duke's Gaffe

SIR – For anyone familiar with India, as I am, it is difficult to comprehend the outcry which has greeted the Duke of Edinburgh's so-called "gaffe" in referring to some electrical wiring as looking as if it had been "put in by an Indian".

Those of us who have spent many years in the sub-continent will be only too familiar with the lax practices of the native electricians, or fusebox wallahs, as they were affectionately known.

I well remember an incident in Madras in 1927 when the lamp on our bridge table began to flicker during a particularly tense rubber involving my wife Mrs Gussett, as she then was, the late Akond of Swat, an old family friend, and his delightful wife, the Anakonda.

I had just bid two no trumps, when suddenly the afore-mentioned light went out completely as its bulb exploded, showering the four of us with tiny shards of glass.

We at once summoned our local fusebox wallah, a Mr Chauduri, who dutifully disappeared into the cupboard under the stairs with his "bag of tricks". After several hours of tinkering with the complicated wiring, while we continued our game with the aid of a hurricane lamp, somewhat incommoded by the huge pink moths which flew around our table in droves, attracted by the unaccustomed brilliance of the kerosene-powered device, Mr Chauduri emerged with a cry of triumph.

"Everything now Number One and A-OK, Gussett Sahib," he confidently reported, with a toothless grin.

I went to the door to switch on the lights, but no sooner had I done so than most of India was plunged into darkness, much to the amusement of our friendly fusebox wallah.

"Oh dear, Sahib!" he cried. "I fear I have connected you to the national grid. Oh my goodness gracious! This will never do!"

Such an incident, by no means untypical, will no doubt have been familiar to the Duke, whose mother-in-law, it must be remembered, was Empress of India and whose uncle "Dickie" Mountbatten was no stranger to the vice-regal lodge at Simla.

H. GUSSETT,
The Old LEB Showrooms,
Wattage,
Oxon.

"Thank you for choosing this pavement. We hope you have enjoyed your journey"

How to annoy James Bond

Late News

WALES HARPOONED OFF GREECE

Greenpeace Protest

THE ONLY known Wales to have swum in Greek waters was attacked yesterday, writes our Greek correspondent *Taki Takalotofcokupthenos.*

A group of hunters equipped with harpoons spotted the Wales disporting himself with his mate in the shallow water off the island of Corfuwataschorchos.

The Wales was spouting about organic vegetables when the hunters cried out "There she blows", believed to be a rude reference to his mate.

However, the Wales, known as Mopy Dick due to his bad temper, swam to safety, leaving the harpoonists empty-handed.

(Reuters)

TV Highlights

Twins
(BBC2)

TONIGHT'S episode features the bizarre case of the Winston twins. One is a hard-working and respected gynaecologist who has been given a seat in the House of Lords. The other is a self-promoting twit who will do anything to get on television. What is uncanny is that they both have identical ridiculous moustaches and silly glasses. What is the link? Are they clones – or clowns?

BLONDE WOMAN WHO WAS GOING TO GET MARRIED CHANGES MIND

by Tara Boomdiaye

A BLONDE woman who had planned to marry her fiancé has broken it off, saying she didn't want to get married after all. Said a close friend of the woman who was going to be wed: "It looks as if she won't be getting married after all."

**NOT ON OTHER PAGES
40,000 die in earthquake.**

HAGUE PLANS FOR RE-LAUNCH

by Our Advertising Staff **Hargleby, Bogleby and Pratt**

AN AUTUMN re-launch is being planned to boost the flagging popularity of William Hague, the Conservative leader.

Since the product came to the market two years ago with a good deal of hype, consumer groups across the board have shown a marked resistance to Hague.

"We simply cannot move him as he is now," says marketing director Amanda Platell, of Bollocks and Crapp. "Nothing short of a complete makeover will get the sales graph upwardly mobile."

Waste of Time

The new campaign, planned by Platell and her colleague Ffion Jenkins, will centre on presenting the product as "cuddly, casual and tactile".

High on the Platell-Jenkins list of priorities are:

● changing name to "Billy Hug". This emphasises both casual and tactile at the same time;

● hair implant, to replace "unfriendly bald image";

● Des Lynam-style moustache to make him look more like ITV's popular new star Des Lynam.

Photo-opportunities for the new-look Hague include:

● visiting fish-and-chip shop in Yorkshire to emphasise Yorkshire roots;

● congratulating lottery winner Aunt Freda Hague and patting her dog, to show closeness to family *(have we got her address?)*;

● appearing on ITV as football anchorman.

HOW HE WILL LOOK

Before

After

HOW SHOULD WE REMEMBER HER?

IT IS two days since the nation was plunged into irreversible grief at the news of the death of Tara Palmer Tomkinson's engagement to Gregory Martin.

One minute she was a happy, smiling, carefree woman who seemed to embody all the hopes and aspirations of a generation of young women. Her face on the front of a magazine was guaranteed to make readers ask "Who's that?" *(Surely "Sell a million copies?" Ed.)*

● How then should we commemorate this beautiful, bewitching, tortured, charismatic *(Get on with it. Ed.)*

Here are the top ten suggestions so far to ensure that Tara's name lives for ever.

1. Commemorative restaurant in Sloane Square to be named "Chez Tara".

2. Equestrian statue of Tara to occupy the empty plinth in Trafalgar Square.

3. Memorial tree to be planted in Kew Gardens by the Duke of Edinburgh.

4. Tara Day, August 24th, to become a national holiday *(England and Wales only)*.

5. Sir Elton John to perform special commemorative song in Westminster Abbey, "I'm not getting married in the morning".

6. Tower of London to be renamed "Tara London".

7. Er...

8. That's it.

The following dignitaries have agreed to sit on the Memorial Committee and have an agreeable lunch *(Surely "decide on a suitable memorial"? Ed.)*: Lord Deedes, Lord Jenkins, Simon Jenkins, Lord Rees-Mogg, Sir Paul Condon, the Archbishop of Canterbury and Dame Joanna Lumley.

95

PASSPORT FOR PETS